COMPUTER
SPORTS
MATCHUPS

COMPUTER SPORTS MATCHUPS

DR. JULIAN E. COMPTON

with BRUCE M. NASH

tempo
books
GROSSET & DUNLAP
A Filmways Company
Publishers • New York

COMPUTER SPORTS MATCHUPS

Copyright © 1981 by Dr. Julian E. Compton with
   Bruce M. Nash
All Rights Reserved
ISBN: 0-448-17249-6

A Tempo Books Original
Tempo Books is registered in the U.S. Patent Office
Printed in the United States of America
Published simultaneously in Canada

Grateful acknowledgment is made for use of the following
material:
    The Afterword is based on the article "Data Boxing: A
Means of Ranking the All-Time Greats" by Julian E.
Compton in *Boxing Illustrated* Vol. 19, No. 12, December,
1977, pp. 38-43. Reprinted by permission of Fax Publishing.

Dedicated to:

Lynn and Woody—each sports in their own way, Bruce Nash, Arnold Kalnitsky, John L. Borchert, and Joe Mastrovito—for helping with the project, all table top sports game players—who play more than the athletes themselves and have more fun at it, too:

The Special Olympians—who are better than the best, because they give their all in arenas beyond the glory of man.

And to:

Jimmy Graham, with fond memories of all our childhood sports "dream matchups."

Contents

Introduction: The All-Time Championships

The guys in the bar were screaming and hollering. Chants of "Ali, Ali" filled the air. Others turned and walked away. They had obviously bet on George Foreman.

The chatter continued after the fight:

"He's got to be the greatest; he knocked out Big George."

"He sure can take a punch."

"He psyched him out."

And then a barroom philosopher with a nose for history declared, "He must be the best heavyweight of all-time. He's the fastest; he's the biggest; he's a legend in his own time."

But a skeptic answered sharply, "He's good; but he wouldn't have been a match for Dempsey." To which, another diehard retorted, "Don't forget Joe Louis. He was Champ for eleven years." And, as the "what if" arguing continued into the night, it became clear that the question of "who was the greatest," is always on the mind of the sports fan.

In baseball's bleachers they might ask, "Needing three runs, with two on and two out, who would you want batting for you?" In Boston the answer is Ted Williams, in New York it's Ruth or DiMaggio, and in Detroit, who else but Ty Cobb.

Around the paddock, claims are made for Citation or Whirlaway, the latter day Secretariat or the old-timer Man o' War, as the one true super horse.

The talk goes on. The sports fan is the ultimate dreamer. He can see the whole event in his mind—the sudden KO, the homer in the ninth, the come-from-behind stretch drive. He

1

makes up ''dream matchups'' in his favorite sport, and works out the winner.

And if the fan can do it in his mind, why can't it be done for real? Why couldn't one get together a bunch of experts in a sport and let them figure out who would win in certain all-time dream matchups? Better yet, if the statistics are available, why not throw them all into a computer, and let it decide who is best in a particular sport?

Well, surprise! It's already been done. Few died-in-the-wool sports fans realize it, but every day some 500,000 sports fans with an interest in games and statistics are replaying their favorite matchups. This book, *Computer Sports Matchups*, is a product of all of that activity.

The All-Time Championships will not answer every ''what if'' question that can be raised about sports. But they will go a long way toward establishing the best teams and individuals in the major events of the sports world.

Here, presented for the first time, are computer-based playoffs for all of the major team and individual sports. Although they are introduced in a non-technical manner, and intended for your enjoyment, they should not be taken lightly. The playoffs are based on research that, in some sports, has been going on for more than twenty years. If you are interested in the technical aspects of the research and analysis, consult the Afterword.

It's time to let your imagination run free, and, by the magic of the computer, attend the greatest events in the dream world of sport. All the legends of sport history are ready to compete for you. As they square off, you might want to predict which ones will emerge as the All-Time Best in each sport. But whether you try to predict or just want to follow the winners, get ready to enjoy sport's greatest moments, even if they are—only a dream.

The All-Time Baseball World Series

The Field

Baseball is called the national pastime. It conjures up more nostalgia and memories than any other sport. Its history is loaded with such legendary stars as Babe Ruth, Ty Cobb, Walter Johnson and Christy Mathewson. Its famous teams include the New York Giants and Yankees, the Boston Red Sox, St. Louis Cardinals, the Detroit Tigers, and the Dodgers of Brooklyn and Los Angeles.

Teams from all the major cities have caught pennant fever since the two leagues were organized in 1901. In 1903, Cy Young led the Boston Red Sox to victory over the Pittsburgh Pirates during the first World Series. Since then, winning the World Series has been the goal of every baseball team. In this all-time playoff, all the pennant winners since 1901 have been evaluated for possible participation. Of the many great teams that have appeared in baseball history, eight were judged as truly superior and worthy to compete in the all-time World Series. Here is a preview of the eight super teams:

1927 New York Yankees (110-44).

They are the most famous team in baseball history. This was the year that Ruth hit his record 60 home runs. Add to that achievement Lou Gehrig's 47 homers and 52 league-leading doubles, as well as Earle Combs' league-leading 231 hits and 23 triples and you have baseball's all-time slugging leaders with a .489 average. The Yankees had a team batting average of .307 and a pitching staff with a 3.20 earned run average. It produced a .714 winning percentage, the best in this field of eight teams. The team won the 1927 Series, beating Pittsburgh in four straight games, and repeated their accomplishment the following year.

Miller Huggins, Manager

Combs	CF	.356	
Koenig	SS	.285	
Ruth	RF	.356	
Gehrig	1B	.373	
Meusel	LF	.337	
Lazzeri	2B	.309	
Dugan	3B	.269	
Collins	C	.275	
Hoyt	22-7	2.64	
Moore	19-7	2.28	
Pennock	19-8	3.00	
Shocker	18-6	2.84	
Ruether	13-6	3.38	
Pipgras	10-3	4.12	

1931 Philadelphia Athletics (107-45).

They broke the Yankees' string, winning the pennant and series in 1929 and '30. They repeated the pennant, but lost the series to the Cardinals in 1931. Connie Mack possessed a true all-star lineup with Al Simmons hitting .390 to lead the league. Jimmie Foxx pounded 30 homers, and Jimmy Dykes and Mickey Cochrane played key roles. The team had three twenty game winners, led by Lefty Grove who won 31. The team batted .287 and had a team E.R.A. of 3.47.

Connie Mack, Manager

Bishop	2B	.294
Haas	CF	.323
Cochrane	C	.349
Simmons	LF	.390
Foxx	1B	.291
Miller	RF	.281
Dykes	3B	.273
Williams	SS	.269

Grove	31-4	2.05
Earnshaw	21-7	3.67
Walberg	20-12	3.74
Mahaffey	15-4	4.22
Hoyt	10-5	4.22

The 1934 St. Louis Cardinals (95-58).

The Gas House Gang had a famous infield, including Frankie Frisch, Leo Durocher, and Pepper Martin. But it was first baseman Rip Collins, hitting 35 homers, who led their hitting attack. Dizzy and Daffy Dean led the pitching staff, which overhauled the Giants with two games left in the season. The Cardinals lost the Series in seven games to Detroit and failed to win the pennant the next year. The team batted .288 and had an E.R.A. of 3.69.

Frankie Frisch, Manager

Martin	3B	.289
Rothrock	RF	.284
Frisch	2B	.305
Medwick	LF	.319
Collins	1B	.333
Davis	C	.300
Orsatti	CF	.300
Durocher	SS	.260

D. Dean	30-7	2.65
P. Dean	18-11	3.44
Carleton	16-11	4.26
Walker	12-4	3.12
Hallahan	8-12	4.25
D. Vance (Relief)	1-1	3.66

1936 New York Yankees (102-51).

It was the first year for the Yankee Clipper, Joe DiMaggio, and he hit .323 with 29 homers. Catcher Bill Dickey hit .362, and Gehrig hit .354, with 49 homers. With a team batting average of .300, they took the pennant by 19½ games. Their team E.R.A.—4.17—was respectable in an age of big hitting; Red Ruffing and Monte Pearson were their top winners. The Yankees had the most enduring dynasty of these eight great final teams, winning the Series from 1936 through 1939.

Joe McCarthy, Manager

Crosetti	SS	.288
Rolfe	3B	.319
DiMaggio	LF	.323
Gehrig	1B	.354
Dickey	C	.362
Selkirk	RF	.308
Powell	CF	.306
Lazzeri	2B	.287
Ruffing	20-12	3.85
Pearson	19-7	3.71
Hadley	14-4	4.34
Gomez	13-7	4.38
Broaca	12-7	4.24

1948 Cleveland Indians (97-58).

In a great pennant race, the Yankees finished two and a half games back, while Cleveland and Boston tied. In a one game playoff, player-manager Lou Boudreau hit two homers as the Indians won 8-3. The Indians took Boston in six series games, executing their first win since 1920. The team batted .283, with Joe Gordon hitting 32 homers, and Ken Keltner 31. The team featured black players Larry Doby and Satchel Paige. Gene Bearden, Bob Lemon, and fireballer Bob Feller were three strong starting pitchers who helped make their team E.R.A. 3.23.

Lou Boudreau, Manager

Mitchell	LF	.336
Clark	RF	.310
Boudreau	SS	.355
Gordon	2B	.280
Keltner	3B	.297
Doby	CF	.301
Robinson	1B	.254
Hegan	C	.248
Bearden	20-7	2.43
Lemon	20-14	2.82
Feller	19-15	3.57
Gromek	9-3	2.84
Paige	6-1	2.47

1955 Brooklyn Dodgers (98-55).

The perennial bridesmaids of 1949, '52, '53 and '56, broke a six-year domination of Yankee teams and won it all in 1955. Power was their game, with 201 home runs spread among Snider (42), Campanella (32), Hodges (27), and Furillo (26). The team hit .271 and had an E.R.A. of 3.68. Their chief pitchers were starter Don Newcombe and reliever Clem Labine.

Walt Alston, Manager

Gilliam	2B	.249
Reese	SS	.282
Snider	CF	.309
Campanella	C	.318
Hodges	1B	.289
Furillo	RF	.314
Robinson	3B	.256
Amoros	LF	.247
Newcombe	20-5	3.19
Erskine	11-8	3.78

Loes	10-4	3.59
Podres	9-10	3.96
Labine	13-5	3.25
(Relief)		

1961 New York Yankees (109-53).

It was a year of broken records. Roger Maris hit 61 homers, breaking Ruth's record. The Yankees hit 240 homers, a figure unmatched by any team. And, in the series, which the Yankees took from the Reds four games to one, Whitey Ford broke Ruth's consecutive scoreless innings record with 32. Although batting only .263, the Yankees got 54 homers from Mantle and 20 or more from four others—Skowron, Berra, Howard and Blanchard. The sound pitching staff, led by Ford at 25-4, had an E.R.A. of 3.46. The Yankees repeated their series win in 1962.

Ralph Houk, Manager

Richardson	2B	.261
Kubek	SS	.276
Maris	RF	.269
Mantle	CF	.317
Howard	C	.348
Skowron	1B	.267
Berra	LF	.271
Boyer	3B	.224
Ford	25-4	3.21
Terry	16-3	3.16
Stafford	14-9	2.68
Coates	11-5	3.45
Sheldon	11-5	3.59
Arroyo	15-5	2.19
(Relief)		

1976 Cincinnati Reds (102-60).

They were called the Big Red Machine because they made winning look so mechanically easy. The team won the series in 1975 and repeated in 1976, beating the Yankees in four straight. The Reds could field, hit for average (.280), and run the bases. Their pitching was not great, as indicated by a team E.R.A. of 3.51. However, this situation was well handled by Manager Sparky Anderson, who was called Captain Hook because he jerked his starters for well-used, sparkling relievers, Rawley Eastwick and Pedro Borbon. The Yankees started Cincinnati's breakup by signing their sometimes healthy Don Gullet as a free agent after the Series.

Sparky Anderson, Manager

Rose	3B	.323
Griffey	RF	.336
Morgan	2B	.320
Perez	1B	.260
Foster	LF	.306
Bench	C	.234
Geronimo	CF	.307
Concepcion	SS	.281
Nolan	15-9	3.46
Zachry	14-7	2.74
Norman	12-7	3.10
Billingham	12-10	4.32
Gullett	11-3	3.00
Eastwick	11-5	2.08
Borbon	4-3	3.35

Here are the pairings for the All-Time World Series.

1936 N.Y. Yankees vs. 1955 Brooklyn Dodgers
1934 St. Louis Cardinals vs. 1976 Cincinnati Reds
1948 Cleveland Indians vs. 1961 N.Y. Yankees
1927 N.Y. Yankees vs. 1931 Philadelphia Athletics

Who will win the All-Time Series? Judging by popular opinion, the Yankees of 1927 and 1961 should be considered the favorites. Both are powerful teams that only the Dodgers can rival in home run production. Unfortunately, both Yankee teams are in the same bracket and cannot meet in the finals. Will the top-hitting 1936 Yankees show well in this competition? Perhaps the balanced play of the Reds will be an advantage. The best pitching seems to belong to the 1927 Yankees and the 1948 Indians. Now that you know about the eight super teams, who do you pick as the All-Time Best?

The Playoffs

First Round: 1936 Yankees vs. 1955 Dodgers

	R	H	E	
36 Yankees	13	20	0	W-Ruffing
55 Dodgers	12	21	0	L-Newcombe

In a slugfest, Gehrig and Dickey homered for the Yankees, Snider for the Dodgers. Yankee reliever Johnny Murphy walked in the twelfth Dodger run in the eighth, but then stopped them for the win.

	R	H	E	
55 Dodgers	7	10	2	L-Erskine
36 Yankees	12	17	0	W-Pearson

Bill Dickey had three doubles and four RBI's to lead the Yankee win. The Dodgers rallied for five runs in the ninth, led by a three-run Campanella homer, but fell short.

	R	H	E	
36 Yankees	7	10	2	W-Gomez
55 Dodgers	5	12	0	L-Podres

Two Snider homers and one by Campanella gave the Dodgers an early lead. Timely singles gave the Yankees four runs in the last three innings, sweeping the series, three games to none.

First Round: 1976 Reds vs. 1934 Cardinals

	R	H	E	
76 Reds	2	4	0	W-Zachary
34 Cardinals	1	5	2	L-Dizzy Dean

Homers by Bob Foster and Bill DeLancey made it 1-1 until the ninth. Then, with two on in the ninth, Cardinal leftfielder Ducky Medwick dropped a Geronimo fly, allowing Foster to score the winning run.

	R	H	E	
34 Cardinals	3	8	2	L-Carleton
76 Reds	5	10	1	W-Norman

Cesar Geronimo went four-for-four, with a double and a homer to lead the Reds' victory.

	R	H	E	
76 Reds	4	7	0	W-Gullett
34 Cardinals	3	9	2	L-Paul Dean

The Reds scored four runs in the first inning, and they were enough. Don Gullett scattered nine hits, striking out seven for the win.

The Reds' defense provided the edge, as the modern team beat the old-timers, three games to none.

Rirst Round: 1961 Yankees vs. 1948 Indians

	R	H	E	
61 Yankees	7	14	1	W-Ford
48 Indians	4	10	1	L-Feller

Although the Indians scored with homers from Joe Gordon and Ken Keltner, the Yankees got the win. Mickey Mantle and Tony Kubek doubled in a three-run seventh and iced the game.

	R	H	E	
48 Indians	8	10	2	W-Lemon
61 Yankees	7	9	1	L-Terry

Allie Clarke's two homers—one a grand slam—put the game out of reach for the Indians. Yogi Berra's ninth inning homer made it close, but reliever Russ Christopher put out the fire.

	R	H	E	
61 Yankees	4	6	0	W-Sheldon
48 Indians	3	9	1	L-Klieman

Gordon's homer provided all the Indian runs. Mantle, Blanchard and Boyer homered for the Yankees. Boyer's eleventh inning run won the game.

	R	H	E	
48 Indians	1	14	1	L-Feller
61 Yankees	3	5	0	W-Ford

Ford scattered 14 hits, aided by a line-out triple play to Boyer in the fourth, for the clincher.

Timely hitting and two Ford wins led to the Yankee victory for the series, three games to one.

First Round: 1927 Yankees vs. 1931 Athletics

	R	H	E	
27 Yankees	5	8	0	W-Hoyt
31 Athletics	3	8	0	L-Walberg

With the game tied in the ninth, Ben Paschal pinch-hit, doubling in two runs for the Yankee win.

	R	H	E	
31 Athletics	6	14	1	L-Grove
27 Yankees	9	15	0	W-Shocker

The Yankees exploded for five runs in the eighth to seal the victory. Collins for the Yankees and Bishop for the Athletics had homers.

	R	H	E	
27 Yankees	6	11	0	W-Pennock
31 Athletics	2	7	1	L-Earnshaw

The Yankees led throughout. A two-run homer by Collins in the ninth put the game out of the Athletics' reach.

Late inning surges took the series for the Yankees, three games to none.

Semifinal: 1927 Yankees vs. 1961 Yankees

	R	H	E	
27 Yankees	12	13	2	W-Hoyt
61 Yankees	2	8	0	L-Stafford

The '27 Yankees put across nine runs in the eighth inning to ice the win.

	R	H	E	
27 Yankees	6	12	2	L-Moore
61 Yankees	7	13	0	W-Arroyo

With two out in the bottom of the ninth, Yogi Berra's pinch-hit single off reliever Wilcy Moore brought home Howard and Blanchard for a dramatic win that tied the series.

	R	H	E	
61 Yankees	3	8	0	L-Terry
27 Yankees	4	8	4	W-Pennock

The old-timers overcame four errors to win. Singles by Koenig and Dugan, a double by Collins, and a sacrifice fly by Meusel scored three runs in the seventh for the victory, resulting in a 2-1 series lead.

	R	H	E	
61 Yankees	5	10	1	W-Sheldon
27 Yankees	3	7	1	L-Moore

Doubles by Kubek and Mantle scored the winning run in the ninth, as Ruth's team failed to hit when needed.

	R	H	E	
61 Yankees	5	7	0	W-Coates
27 Yankees	4	4	1	L-Pipgras

The '61 Yankees took a 3-2 series lead by beating the '27 Yankees at their own power game. Five solo homers, two each by Mantle and Berra and one by Blanchard, supplied all the runs. Although Stafford allowed only two hits through seven innings, the old-timers led until Mantle and Berra homered in the ninth for the win.

	R	H	E	
27 Yankees	8	16	2	W-Pennock
61 Yankees	3	11	0	L-Ford

Ruth and Gehrig had solo homers in the third, but the score held at 2-2 when Ford departed in the eighth. Relievers Clevenger and Daley were overwhelmed, and the '27 Yankees evened the series.

	R	H	E	
27 Yankees	5	13	1	W-Shocker
61 Yankees	2	7	1	L-Terry

Three runs in the fifth, capped by Bob Meusel's double, put the game out of reach. Maris had a homer for the losers.

Four complete games by the 1927 pitchers, including two by Pennock, seemed to be the edge in this close series. Meusel's consistent hitting eclipsed the bigger bats of both teams and contributed to the win. The 1927 Yankees defeat the 1961 Yankees four games to three.

Semifinal: 1976 Reds vs. 1936 Yankees

	R	H	E	
76 Reds	8	9	0	W-Eastwick
36 Yankees	6	14	1	L-Ruffing

Morgan for the Reds and Gehrig for the Yankees had homers. But the game was won by Ed Armbrister's pinch-hit double, which scored three runs in the ninth.

	R	H	E	
76 Reds	10	11	0	W-Zachary
36 Yankees	7	16	1	L-Pearson

The Yankees had sixteen hits, six walks, and homers by Selkirk and Crosetti. The Reds offset this with a timely defense and the two double, five RBI performance by Dave Concepcion, and went up 2-0 in games.

	R	H	E	
36 Yankees	1	5	0	L-Gomez
76 Reds	2	10	1	W-Norman

Rose and Griffey scored all runs the Reds needed in the first then held on to overcome Dickey's ninth inning homer.

	R	H	E	
36 Yankees	5	9	0	W-Broaca
76 Reds	2	5	0	L-Gullett

Gehrig and Morgan traded third inning homers. But Crosetti's three hits and Broaca's nine strikeouts gave the Yankees their first win.

	R	H	E	
36 Yankees	1	4	0	L-Ruffing
76 Reds	2	6	2	W-Borbon

In the seventh, Foster tripled, Geronimo walked and Bench singled them in for the series win. The Yankees' only run came on pitcher Red Ruffing's homer.

In a mild surprise, the 1976 Cincinnati Reds have eased their way into the finals. In getting the win, Reds' Manager Sparky Anderson maintained his "Captain Hook" image by constantly jerking his starting pitchers. The 1976 Reds defeat the 1936 Yankees, four games to one.

Final: 1927 Yankees vs. 1976 Reds
(Best 5 out of 9 game series)

	R	H	E	
76 Reds	3	7	1	L-Nolan
27 Yankees	8	13	0	W-Hoyt

Yankee homers by Dugan, Hoyt, and Koenig more than overcame Foster's solo round-tripper, as Yankee power overwhelmed Nolan.

	R	H	E	
27 Yankees	6	10	0	W-Pennock
76 Reds	0	6	0	L-Zachary

Collins and Ruth hit homers and Pennock shut out the Reds as the Yankees took a 2-0 lead.

	R	H	E	
27 Yankees	3	11	3	L-Moore
76 Reds	6	12	0	W-Eastwick

Three Reds' singles and a Koenig error at short let in three eighth inning runs, and gave the Reds their first win.

	R	H	E	
76 Reds	3	8	1	L-Eastwick
27 Yankees	4	13	0	W-Moore

In the eleventh inning, a bases-loaded single by Gehrig gave the Yankees a 3-1 series lead.

	R	H	E	
27 Yankees	18	20	1	W-Hoyt
76 Reds	10	17	1	L-Zachary

Trailing by two after seven innings, the Yankees scored six runs in both the eighth and ninth to demolish the Reds. One more Yankee victory would end the series.

	R	H	E	
76 Reds	8	15	1	L-Nolan
27 Yankees	12	10	0	W-Pennock

The Reds showed power, getting homers from Foster and Driessen. However, the Yankees produced homers from Collins, Gehrig, and two from Dugan, and soundly defeated their challengers to prove they were the best.

John Mosedale wrote a book about them, *The Greatest of All, The 1927 New York Yankees*. The title seems to be right, for they truly were a remarkable team. The Yankees of 1927 have survived in an age of new sports developments that have all but eliminated past greats from consideration as all-time bests. A team from more than fifty years ago has emerged as the all-time champs.

We wish to add a special tribute to Ruth and Gehrig, Combs and Meusel, Hoyt and Moore, Pennock and Shocker and all the rest led by Manager Miller Huggins who reign as the best that ever were.

Individual Batting

1927 New York Yankees

		AB	H	2B	3B	HR	R	RBI	BB	BA
E. Combs	CF	28	7	1	0	0	5	1	5	.250
M. Koenig	SS	31	9	0	0	1	5	4	0	.290
B. Ruth	RF	21	10	2	0	1	8	5	9	.476
L. Gehrig	1B	25	13	5	1	1	7	9	4	.520
B. Meusel	LF	24	5	0	1	0	4	5	2	.208
T. Lazzeri	2B	20	8	2	0	0	7	5	6	.400
J. Dugan	3B	20	6	0	0	3	5	8	1	.300
P. Collins	C	23	7	1	0	2	5	7	3	.304
W. Hoyt	p	7	4	1	0	1	2	3	0	.571
H. Pennock	p	7	1	0	0	0	1	0	1	.143
U. Shocker	p	2	0	0	0	0	0	0	0	.000
D. Reuther	p	3	2	1	0	0	0	0	0	.667
W. Moore	p	2	0	0	0	0	0	0	0	.000
G. Pipgras	p	1	1	0	0	0	0	2	0	1.000
B. Paschal	ph	3	0	0	0	0	0	0	0	.000
M. Gazella	ph, 3B	4	3	0	0	0	1	0	0	.750
R. Morehart	ph	2	1	0	0	0	1	0	0	.500
Team		223	77	13	2	9	51	49	31	.345

1976 Cincinnati Reds

		AB	H	2B	3B	HR	R	RBI	BB	BA
P. Rose	3B	27	11	3	0	0	4	5	1	.407
K. Griffey	RF	25	8	2	0	0	3	3	3	.320
J. Morgan	2B	24	5	0	0	1	6	4	4	.208
B. Foster	LF	27	7	0	0	2	2	6	0	.259
T. Perez	ph,1B	20	4	2	0	0	0	1	0	.200
C. Geronimo	CF	26	7	1	2	0	2	2	1	.269
J. Bench	C	24	6	0	0	0	3	2	3	.250

D. Concepcion	SS	25	11	1	0	0	5	4	0	.440
D. Driessen	ph,1B	11	5	0	0	2	4	3	1	.454
P. Zachary	p	4	1	0	0	0	1	0	0	.250
G. Nolan	p	3	0	0	0	0	0	0	0	.000
D. Gullett	p	1	0	0	0	0	0	0	1	.000
D. Flynn	ph	2	0	0	0	0	0	0	0	.000
B. Bailey	ph	2	0	0	0	0	0	0	0	.000
E. Armbrister	ph	2	0	0	0	0	0	0	0	.000
F. Norman	p	0	0	0	0	0	0	0	0	.000
R. Eastwick	p	0	0	0	0	0	0	0	0	.000
Team		223	65	9	2	5	30	30	14	.291

Individual Pitching

1927 New York Yankees

	W	L	IP	ER	H	BB	SO	ERA
W. Hoyt	2	0	16	11	20	3	6	6.19
H. Pennock	2	0	18	8	21	6	7	4.00
D. Ruether	0	0	7.3	2	6	0	0	2.46
U. Shocker	0	0	6	3	8	0	0	4.50
W. Moore	1	1	5.6	1	6	0	3	1.59
G. Pipgras	0	0	1.6	0	0	0	2	0.00
M. Thomas	0	0	0.3	2	4	0	0	54.55
Team	5	1	55	27	65	9	18	4.42

1976 Cincinnati Reds

	W	L	IP	ER	H	BB	SO	ERA
G. Nolan	0	2	11	17	19	4	5	13.91
P. Zachary	0	1	12.3	15	19	10	11	10.95
D. Gullett	0	0	6	3	7	4	3	4.50
F. Norman	0	0	7	3	10	3	0	3.86
P. Borbon	0	1	4.6	4	8	0	0	7.71
R. Eastwick	1	1	4	1	6	3	3	2.25
W. McEnaney	0	0	4	0	2	2	1	0.00
J. Billingham	0	0	2	2	1	2	0	9.00
D. Alcala	0	0	2	5	5	3	0	22.50
Team	1	5	53	50	77	31	23	8.49

The All-Time Star Baseball Game

The Teams

In 1933, a Grantland Rice idea brought together the All Stars for the first time, with the American League winning 4-2. Now, with those same original managers, we bring together the best players of all-time for a dream game. Surprisingly, thirteen of the original all-stars were chosen to play in this game. The lineups follow:

National League, John McGraw			American League, Connie Mack		
Honus Wagner	SS	.329	Babe Ruth	RF	.342
Rogers Hornsby	2B	.358	Ted Williams	LF	.344
Stan Musial	1B	.331	Joe DiMaggio	CF	.325
Mel Ott	RF	.304	Lou Gehrig	1B	.340
Willie Keeler	LF	.345	Nap Lajoie	2B	.339
Paul Waner	CF	.333	Jimmy Collins	3B	.294
Pie Traynor	3B	.320	Joe Cronin	SS	.302
Roy Campanella	C	.276	Bill Dickey	C	.313
Christy Mathewson	P	W373-L188	Walter Johnson	P	W416-L279

The All-Time All-Star Game boasts the largest collection of all-stars that any sport can assemble. In fact, with the presence of Wee Willie Keeler on the National squad, the players come from as far back as the 1890's.

With so much talent to draw from, many great players did not make the teams. And the benches are fantastic. The National League has Ernie Banks, Jackie Robinson, Bill Terry, Hank Aaron, Eddie Mathews, Willie Mays, Frankie Frisch and Gabby Hartnett on their bench. The American League has Mickey Mantle, Al Simmons, Tris Speaker, George Sisler, Eddie Collins, Lou Boudreau, Yogi Berra, Jimmy Foxx and even Ty Cobb starting out on the bench.

Pitchers for the National League, after their starter Mathewson, include Cy Young, Sandy Koufax, Grover Cleveland Alexander, Ed "Three Finger" Brown, Carl Hubbell, Joe McGinnity, Dizzy Dean and Warren Spahn. The American League, after Johnson, can choose from Ed Walsh, Ed Plank, Rube Waddell, Lefty Grove, Bob Feller, Whitey Ford and Hal Newhouser.

With so much talent, no further introduction is necessary. Here it is—the All-Time All-Star Game.

The National League jumped on Walter Johnson in the first inning for three runs, and went on to win 8-4.

Wagner drew a walk as the game started. Hornsby singled him to third. Musial flied to center, and Wagner tagged up and scored. Ott then doubled, sending Hornsby to third. Keeler singled to center, scoring Hornsby and Ott for a 3-0 lead. Wagner hit into a double play to end the half inning.

Williams homered in the bottom of the first inning, to make it 3-1. The score remained that until Ruth made it 3-2 with a homer in the third. Mathewson had three on as a result of walks after Ruth's homer but got Crosetti to pop up to end the trouble.

In the fourth, Campanella walked and Mathewson sacrificed him to second. He moved to third on a Gehrig error, and scored on a Musial single. That made it 4-2.

In the top of the sixth, Wagner singled and stole second. Hornsby singled him home to make it 5-2. In the bottom of the sixth, the American League came back on a Crosetti single and a homer by Dickey. There was now a 5-4 National lead with three innings to go. It seemed like anyone's game.

In the eighth inning, McGraw started emptying his bench. Frisch hit for Traynor and got on by a Collins error. Hartnett singled, batting for Campanella. Koufax forced Frisch at third, trying to sacrifice. Banks pinch-hit for Wagner and was struck out by Feller. With the game still in doubt,

McGraw left in Hornsby, who had singled three times in four at bats. Hornsby hit a Feller fastball into the left field seats and the National League led 8-4. Koufax held the American League scoreless in the last three innings. With two out and the bases full in the bottom of the ninth, Boudreau popped up and the National League had the victory.

In this game of All-Time All-Stars, the hitters seemed to dominate. Ruth, Williams and Dickey had round-trippers for the American League. But the big star of the game was Rogers Hornsby, who went four for five with one homer and scored twice for the National League.

No pitchers were overwhelming. Cy Young had five strikeouts in the middle three innings. Koufax pitched the only shutout ball, going the last three for the National League.

More timely hitting won it for the National League, as the American League left twelve on base. But the real winners were the fans who saw the best of all-time together in one game. It was a moment of glory that all the participants deserved.

All-Time All-Stars: National At American League

National	AB	R	H	RBI	American	AB	R	H	RBI
Wagner, SS	3	2	1	0	Ruth, RF	4	1	1	1
Banks, ph, SS	1	0	0	0	Mantle, ph, RF	1	0	0	0
Hornsby, 2B	5	2	4	4	Williams, LF	1	1	1	1
Robinson, 2B	0	0	0	0	Simmons, LF	1	0	0	0
Musial, 1B	3	0	1	2	DiMaggio, CF	4	0	0	0
Terry, ph, 1B	1	0	0	0	Speaker, CF	1	0	1	0
Ott, RF	2	1	1	0	Gehrig, 1B	3	0	1	0
Aaron, ph, RF	1	0	0	0	Sisler, 1B	1	0	1	0
Keeler, LF	3	0	2	2	Lajoie, 2B	4	0	1	0
Mathews, ph, LF	2	0	0	0	E. Collins, 2B	1	0	0	0
Waner, CF	4	0	0	0	J. Collins, 3B	3	0	0	0
Mays, ph, CF	1	0	0	0	Cronin, SS	2	1	1	0
Traynor, 3B	3	0	0	0	Boudreau, SS	2	0	0	0

National	AB	R	H	RBI	American	AB	R	H	RBI
Frisch, ph, 3B	1	0	0	0	Dickey, C	3	1	2	2
Campanella, C	3	1	1	0	Berra, ph, C	1	0	0	0
Hartnett, ph, C	1	1	1	0	Johnson, P	1	0	0	0
Mathewson, P	1	0	0	0	Walsh, P	1	0	0	0
Young, P	1	0	0	0	Foxx, ph	1	0	0	0
Koufax, P	1	1	0	0	Feller, P	0	0	0	0
					Cobb, ph	1	0	0	0
					Ford, P	0	0	0	0
Totals	37	8	11	8	Totals	36	4	9	4

```
National    300  101  030—8
American    101  002  000—4
```

National	IP	H	R	ER	BB	SO
Mathewson (W)	3	3	2	2	4	2
Young	3	3	2	2	1	5
Koufax	3	3	0	0	2	3

American	IP	H	R	ER	BB	SO
Johnson (L)	3	6	3	3	2	2
Walsh	3	3	2	1	1	2
Feller	2	2	3	2	1	3
Ford	1	0	0	0	1	0

E—Gehrig, J. Collins
DP—American 2
LOB—National 7, American 12
2B—Ott, Gehrig
HR—Williams, Ruth, Dickey, Hornsby
SB—Wagner
S—Mathewson, Koufax.

The All-Time College Basketball Playoff

The Field

Since Dr. James Naismith nailed up a peach basket in a Springfield, Massachusetts gym in 1891, basketball has been an American sport. It has since become a professional and international sport, but its heartbeat is on the American amateur level.

By the 1920's, college basketball had established itself in the heartland and had begun to appeal to the big cities. The first National Collegiate Athletic Association Tournament was held in 1939, with eight teams participating. Oregon defeated Ohio State in the finals, winning the first title. The college game left its "minor sport" image behind, achieving status through big-city newspaper publicity.

In the early years of the NCAA Tournament, several dynasties dominated the sport. Among these were coach Hank Iba's Oklahoma State team, which won the NCAA in 1945 and '46, Adolph Rupp's Kentucky, which won in 1948, '49 and '51, and Phil Woolpert's San Francisco, which won in 1955 and '56 and achieved a record sixty straight victories.

In the 1960's and '70's, a higher quality of players and competition produced a more wide-open game. Many excellent teams contended for the title each year as the tournament swelled to thirty-two, then forty teams in 1979. However, college basketball also saw the appearance of perhaps the most successful dynasty in all of sports—the UCLA Bruins. Between 1964 and 1973, in a sport where upsets are prevalent and in tournaments where one loss will eliminate a team, UCLA won nine titles in ten years, losing only in 1966. They also won eighty-eight straight games during 1971-74, shattering San Francisco's previous record.

The earlier dynasties will not be represented in this all-time tournament, but UCLA will be. Here is a preview of the sixteen teams which qualified for the tournament. All of them are teams which have played since 1960.

1962 Cincinnati (29-2). Doing what the Oscar Robertson teams of 1958-60 could not do, this Ed Jucker coached team beat Ohio State in the NCAA finals in 1961 and '62 and lost to Loyola (Chicago) in the 1963 finals. They were led by Ron Bonham, Tom Thacker, Tony Yates and Paul Hogue. The team played tenacious defense.

1976 Notre Dame (23-6). Perhaps the best Notre Dame team, they lost only six games against tough competition. Adrian Dantley, Dave Batton and Bruce Flowers were strong underneath, with Duck Williams scoring outside under coach Digger Phelps.

1973 UCLA (30-0). John Wooden's record breakers broke San Francisco's win streak record. Bill Walton and Keith Wilkes (now Jamaal Wilkes) were at the posts, Larry Farmer and Larry Hollyfield on the wings, Tommy Curtis or Greg Lee at the point and Swen Nater, Dave Myers and Pete Trgovich on the bench. They lost in 1974, so this was Walton's best year.

1968 Houston (31-2). Guy Lewis' team beat UCLA and an injured Lew Alcindor (now Kareem Abdul Jabbar) in the Astrodome at mid-season but lost to them in the playoffs, taking third place in the NCAA. Elvin Hayes and Theodis Lee were at forward, Ken Spain at center, Don Chaney and George Reynolds at guard. They stopped the forty-seven game winning streak of a great team 71-69, but lost 101-69 when Alcindor was sound.

1978 Kentucky (30-2). Joe Hall's team broke a twenty-year championship drought for the tradition-laden school. Rick Robey, Mike Phillips, Jack Givens and James Lee underneath with Kyle Macy steadying them at guard, led to a machine-like power approach.

1966 Texas Western (28-1). Don Haskins's team was primarily black, led by Dave Lattin, Bobby Joe Hill, Willie Cager, Orsten Artis, Neville Shed and Willie Worsley. They upset "Rupp's Runts" of Kentucky in the finals and were the only non-UCLA winner between '64 and '73.

1976 Indiana (32-0). Bobby Knight's power team of Kent Benson, Scott May, Quinn Buckner, Bobby Wilkerson and Tom Abernathy—all drafted by the NBA—went undefeated, beating their opponents by an average of seventeen points a game.

1965 Davidson (24-2). Lefty Driesell's high-ranked team was led by Fred Hetzel and Dick Snyder. A one point loss in the Southern Conference finals prevented them from going for the title.

1962 Ohio State (26-2). Fred Taylor's team won in 1960 and were runners up to Cincinnati in '61 and '62. This team was led by John Havlicek, Jerry Lucas and Doug McDonald in the front line, Dick Reasbeck at guard, and Gary Bradds as a substitute.

1977 Marquette (25-7). Al McGuire's last year gave Marquette its first title. Coming off a tough schedule, the team of Bo Ellis, Bruce Lee, Jerome Whitehead, Gary Rosenberger, Jim Boylan and Bernard Toone played a patterned offense with great success.

1972 Florida State (27-6). Hugh Durham's surprise independent team went to the finals against UCLA. Reggie Royals, Roland Garret and Lawrence McCray in front, with Ron King shooting and Gene Harris or Greg Samuel as play-maker, engaged UCLA in one of their closest contests, losing 81-76.

1968 UCLA (29-1). One of Wooden's best, they lost only to Houston in the Astrodome in mid-season with Jabbar (Alcindor) ailing. Lynn Shackelford, Lucius Allen, Mike

Warren, Edgar Lacey and Mike Lynn joined the big man on a great team that put away Houston and North Carolina in the finals.

1963 Loyola (29-2). George Ireland used four black starters, averaging over ninety points a game, and lifted the championship from Cincinnati in overtime. Jerry Harkness was the big star, backed by John Egan, Les Hunter, Ron Miller and Vic Rouse.

1977 North Carolina (25-4). Dean Smith's team was supposed to win as his U.S. Olympic team had done in 1976. However, the balance of Mike O'Koren, Walter Davis, Tom LaGarde, Phil Ford, and John Kuester and the slow-down "four corners" attack ran out of gas in the finals against Marquette.

1970 Jacksonville (27-2). Joe Williams started the two seven-footers Artis Gilmore and Pembrook Burrows, with Rod McIntyre on the front line and Roy Wedeking and Rex Morgan in backcourt. They went up nine on UCLA early in the finals, but tapered off and lost 80-69.

1974 North Carolina State (30-1). Norm Sloan's 1973 team was undefeated but banned from post-season play, which UCLA won. They met early in 1974 on a neutral court, the two undefeateds battling for last year's title, with UCLA winning by sixteen. Later in the '74 NCAA semifinals UCLA blew an eleven point lead; State won in double overtime and then beat Marquette 76-64 in the finals. David Thompson and seven-footer Tom Burleson were the stars, backed by Monty Towe, Phil Spence, Moe Rivers and Tim Stoddard.

The tournament shapes up as a question of, "Who can take it from UCLA?" Under John Wooden, this team won the NCAA ten times in twelve years. While UCLA is the only school with two teams in the tournament, it still probably is underrepresented. However, both of its entries are strong teams with plenty of depth. One team is led by Lew Alcindor (Jabbar); the other, by Bill Walton. Jacksonville's Artis

Gilmore is probably the only center in the tournament who can play even with the UCLA giants in both scoring and rebounding. But his team is probably not as strong as he.

Strong balanced teams that might challenge UCLA include: Loyola, which boasts high scoring and good rebounding; Indiana, with a one-two punch in Scott May and Ken Benson; Kentucky, with scorers Rick Robey and Jack Givens; and Houston, probably the best rebounding team in the tournament. Houston also boasts Elvin Hayes, the most powerful forward on any team.

Will the winner be UCLA, another power team, or will a surprise team emerge? On with the tourney.

The Pairings

1962 Cincinnati (29-2)
vs.
1976 Notre Dame (23-6)

1973 UCLA (30-0)
vs.
1968 Houston (31-2)

1978 Kentucky (30-2)
vs.
1966 Texas Western (28-1)

1976 Indiana (32-0)
vs.
1965 Davidson (24-2)

1962 Ohio State (26-2)
vs.
1977 Marquette (25-7)

1972 Florida State (27-6)
vs.
1968 UCLA (29-1)

1963 Chicago Loyola (29-2)
vs.
1977 North Carolina (25-4)

1970 Jacksonville (27-2)
vs.
1974 North Carolina State (30-1)

The Playoffs

First Round: 1962 Cincinnati 83, 1976 Notre Dame 78

Cincinnati held off a second-half charge by Notre Dame to win. The Fighting Irish, led by Adrian Dantley and Dave Batton, wiped out a 50-40 Bearcat lead to tie at 60-all with 11:15 remaining in the game. Key baskets by Wilson and Bonham ended the threat. Bonham's 22 and Yates' 20 led the winners while Dantley had 25 and Batton scored 21 for the losers.

First Round: 1973 UCLA 84, 1968 Houston 79

Houston's superior rebounding was offset by a razor-sharp UCLA defense in a game in which the momentum shifted continually. During the final four minutes, Houston closed to within three points five times. Balanced UCLA scoring, led by Bill Walton's 21 points, contributed to the UCLA win.

First Round: 1978 Kentucky 83, 1966 Texas Western 77

Fouling hurt Texas Western in the late stages of the game, and Kentucky swept to victory in overtime. Both Neil Shed and Dave Lattin were lost in the last three minutes of regulation time, and Bobby Joe Hill fouled out as the overtime period began. Rick Robey's 27 points and 19 by Jack Givens led the Wildcats. Artis had 24 for the losers.

First Round: 1976 Indiana 76, 1965 Davidson 71

Indiana almost blew a sixteen-point lead in winning a first round game over Davidson. The Wildcat charge began in earnest with seven minutes left and Indiana holding a 70-56 lead. With five seconds remaining in the game the Hoosiers held a 74-71 lead and held on to win. Scott May scored 30 for Indiana, but Dick Snyder had 34 points for Davidson.

First Round: 1977 Marquette 80, 1962 Ohio State 78

Marquette was losing to Ohio State by eleven points. But with eight minutes left in the first half, Marquette rallied to win a squeaker. The Warriors led for the first time in the game at 62-60 as Butch Lee fed Gary Rosenberger for two. Ohio State regained the lead three more times before baskets by Jerome Whitehead and Bo Ellis gave Marquette a four point cushion and the game. Lee's 22 and Jim Boylan's 21 overcame the 32 points that Jerry Lucas put in for the losing Buckeyes.

First Round: 1968 UCLA 74, 1972 Florida State 72

After a 4-all tie, Florida State fell back until a rally in the second half put them ahead 42-41. However, baskets by Lew Alcindor, Lucius Allen and Mike Lynn, ended the threat to UCLA. Down 72-62 with 3:25 remaining in the game, Florida State charged again to close within two points at the buzzer. Alcindor had 22 to lead UCLA, but Ron King led all scorers with 27 points.

First Round: 1963 Chicago Loyola 69, 1977 North Carolina 68

At the buzzer, Jerry Harkness was fouled while shooting by North Carolina's Tommy Lagarde. Harkness missed his first attempt, then watched the second bounce on the rim before dropping through and giving Chicago Loyola victory by a point. The Tar Heels, who trailed most of the game, scored four baskets in ninety seconds to lead 63-55 with 5:50 left in the game. However, Loyola fought back and were leading 65-64 with 1:40 remaining. John Kuester's tap-in tied the score with five seconds left and set the stage for

Harkness' dramatic foul conversion. Phil Ford fouled out during the game-ending Loyola rally and finished with 16 points. Vic Rouse scored 18 for Loyola to lead all scorers.

First Round: 1970 Jacksonville 90, 1974 North Carolina State 80

Jacksonville trailed 46-41 with two minutes remaining in the half, but rallied to take a 47-46 lead into the locker room. The team continued the momentum in the second half to defeat North Carolina State. David Thompson scored 28 points for the Wolfpack, but Artis Gilmore had 31 to lead Jacksonville. Vaughn Wedeking contributed 26 for the winners.

Quarter-Final: 1973 UCLA 72, 1962 Cincinnati 58

Two of the best defensive teams of the tournament met, but UCLA jumped into a 28-8 lead after twelve minutes and Cincinnati had to play catch up during the remainder of the game. The Bearcats closed to 53-45 with twelve minutes left in the contest, but UCLA pulled away to win. Bill Walton's 31 points led all scorers while Paul Hogue had 21 for Cincinnati.

Quarter-Final: 1976 Indiana 71, 1978 Kentucky 59

Indiana jumped to a 31-16 lead during the first fifteen minutes of the first half and maintained a comfortable margin throughout. Scott May scored 19 of his game-leading points in the second half, helping to maintain the Hoosiers' momentum. Jack Givens was limited to six points in the second half and finished with 15.

Quarter-Final: 1968 UCLA 80, 1977 Marquette 70

UCLA broke open a seesaw battle with eight straight points, taking a 58-50 lead after seven minutes of the second half. The team then held off a final Warrior charge in the closing minutes. The UCLA starting five all scored in double figures. Butch Lee had 22 and Jerome Whitehead 20 for the losing Warriors.

Quarter-Final: 1963 Chicago Loyola 87, 1970 Jacksonville 75

Chicago Loyola lost a thirteen-point lead in the first half, but rallied midway through the last half to pull away from Jacksonville. Ten points by Ron Miller and Jerry Harkness broke a 58-all tie, giving the game to Loyola. Miller led all scorers with 28 points, while Artis Gilmore had 25 for Jacksonville.

Semi-Final: 1973 UCLA 95, 1976 Indiana 75

UCLA received 17 assists and 60 points from Bill Walton and Larry Farmer and, spurting everytime the Hoosiers closed, crushed Indiana. Although Scott May scored 30 points and Kent Benson added 22, UCLA's 45 baskets were too much for the midwestern team.

The contest was close for the first nine minutes as UCLA led 20-18. Then UCLA erupted for eight straight points—four by Walton—and the score became 28-18. After five minutes of the second half, UCLA jumped from a 60-50 lead to a 22-point margin, with Farmer getting eight in the twelve-point run.

Indiana closed for the final time. Tom Abernathy's three-point play got the Hoosiers within 13, at 81-68, with five minutes remaining. Then UCLA finished them off.

Semi-Final: 1968 UCLA 91, 1963 Chicago Loyola 76

UCLA took command at the start, building leads of 20 and 22 points. Chicago Loyola did close to within thirteen points with 4:20 left in the game. Lew Alcindor couldn't be stopped with 19 baskets and 43 points.

Chicago Loyola, led by Jerry Harkness, Vic Rouse, Leslie

Hunter, and Ron Miller, outscored UCLA 44-41 during the second half.

Third Place Game: 1963 Chicago Loyola 92, 1976 Indiana 90

In one of the most thrilling games of the tournament, Chicago Loyola outlasted Indiana—92-90—to win third place. Scott May scored 41 points for Indiana. But the Hoosiers lost the lead with two minutes left on Leslie Hunter's tap-in. Chicago Loyola went on to win. Hunter led Loyola with 30 points.

The lead changed hands fourteen times and the score was tied nine times. Indiana led 80-76 with 4:45 remaining, but Hunter's basket drew Loyola within one, at 86-86, at 2:55. His tap-in, with 2:10 remaining, ended Indiana's hopes.

Final: 1973 UCLA 85, 1968 UCLA 75

1973 UCLA won The All-Time College Basketball Playoffs by defeating the 1968 UCLA club, 85-75. The game was close throughout but was dominated by the 1973 five who had balanced scoring and good shooting.

The sticky defense of the 1973 team hampered the 1968 shooters. The 1973 club played its starters throughout and all were in double figures. Both Bill Walton for the 1973 team and Lew Alcindor for the 1968 club had 19 points.

The 1968 UCLA team jumped to an 8-3 lead in the first two minutes with two baskets by Alcindor. But the 1973 UCLA five moved into the lead at 12-11 when Tommy Curtis fed Bill Walton for two. The lead changed hands again until, with 3:50 remaining in the half, the 1973 team took command. Keith Wilkes scored five points in the scoring flurry, and the 1973 club went to the locker room with a 45-38 halftime lead.

The 1973 team stretched leads to eleven points three times during the second half. Each time the 1968 UCLA five fought back, but ran out of steam during the last six minutes of the game.

Between the two teams, there were 31 assists. The contest was played cleanly with no player fouling out.

1973 UCLA	G	F	Reb	A	T	1968 UCLA	G	F	Reb	A	T
Wilkes	8	4	5	2	20	Lynn	5	0	4	1	10
Farmer	7	1	11	6	15	Shackleford	3	2	12	2	8
Walton	9	1	6	2	19	Alcindor	9	1	5	3	19
Curtis	5	2	8	5	12	Allen	8	0	5	1	16
Hollyfield	8	3	6	1	19	Warren	10	2	12	4	22
TOTALS	37	11	36	16	85	Lacey	0	0	6	4	0
						Sutherland	0	0	1	0	0
						TOTALS	35	5	45	15	75

FOULED OUT: None.
TOTAL FOULS: 1973 UCLA 11, 1968 UCLA 15.
HALFTIME: 1973 UCLA 45, 1968 UCLA 38.

The 1973 UCLA team is the all-time best college basketball team. It's not surprising that a UCLA team won as these teams dominated the sport for a decade. Considering the difficulty of the playoff process in this sport, UCLA's record is the envy of even the Boston Celtics, the New York Yankees, and the Montreal Canadiens dynasties. The UCLA dynasty is, of course, the product of the Wizard of Westwood, John Wooden.

Wooden's ability to put a winner on the court came to its peak in the eras of Lew Alcindor and Bill Walton. These two teams met in the all-time finals and the Walton team won. This squad played great team basketball and sent Walton and Keith Wilkes to the pros. The fact that other teams often send more individual players to the pros, while UCLA keeps on winning, suggests that Wooden is the master of the college game. Our congratulations to John Wooden, UCLA, and all his great players from 1973 or any other season. You are truly great!

The All-Time Professional
Basketball Playoff

The Field

Beginning in the 1920's, pro basketball grew in towns such as Oshkosh, Sheboygan, Akron, Fort Wayne and Indianapolis. By the mid-1940's, big cities, big arenas and a big star, George Mikan, contributed to what became the National Basketball Association. The 24-second shot clock was introduced in 1954, and the league began to build its reputation apart from the college game.

As talent increased, another league appeared. The American Basketball Association existed between 1968 and 1976 and then merged with the N.B.A. In this playoff of the eight best teams of all-time, only two teams from the pre-1968, less-talented years, made the final group. Here is a preview of the eight star-filled teams which will compete for the all-time title.

Boston Celtics 1965. Won 77%. 8.3 Margin.

From 1959-69, Boston lost the NBA title only in 1967. The Celtics' 1965 team is probably their best team from that period. Bill Russell was a rebounding and defensive center. K.C. Jones was a defensive guard. Tom Heinsohn and Tom Sanders were at forward; John Havlicek was a swing-man between guard and forward. And guard Sam Jones supplied the fire power with a 26-point average.

Philadelphia '76ers 1967. Won 84%. 9.4 Margin.

Led by Wilt Chamberlain's 24-point average and guard Hal Greer's 22, the team featured Lucius Jackson, Chet Walker and Billy Cunningham at forward. Wally Jones was the other guard. This team was the only one to beat Boston in an eleven-year span, eliminating them four games to one.

New York Knicks 1970. Won 73%. 9.1 Margin.

The team was led by Willis Reed at center with a 22-point average and Walt Frazier with a 21-point average, a high number of assists and great defense. Dave DeBusschere, Bill Bradley and Dick Barnett rounded out the starting team. They held their opponents eleven below the league average and are probably the best defensive team in the history of pro basketball.

Milwaukee Bucks 1971. Won 81%. 12.2 Margin.

The Bucks were led by Jabbar's 32-point average during the first and best of three great years (1971-73). Bob Dandridge and Greg Smith at forward and Jon McGlocklin at guard were all molded together by the scoring, assists, defense and overall play of Oscar Robertson. They were the first team to shoot over fifty percent.

Los Angeles Lakers 1972. Won 84%. 12.3 Margin.

Jerry West and Gail Goodrich each averaged 26 a game at guard. Wilt Chamberlain was content to rebound, along with Happy Hairston at forward, while Jim McMillan was the scoring forward. Flynn Robinson, LeRoy Ellis, and Keith Erickson gave good bench strength. They have the best win percent and scoring margin in NBA history.

Kentucky Colonels 1972 (ABA). Won 84%. 9.0 Margin.

Forward Dan Issel's 31-point average and Artis Gilmore's 24 at center, along with forward Cincy Powell (16), Louie Dampier (16) and Darrell Carrier (14) gave the Colonels a scoring machine. Theirs was the best season in ABA history, but a Carrier injury prevented the Kentucky team from winning the playoffs. Walt Simon was a good forward off the bench.

Boston Celtics 1973. Won 83%. 8.2 Margin.

A mobile team, the Celtics had Dave Cowens (20.5 average) at center, Paul Silas and Don Nelson at forward, JoJo

White (20) at guard, with John Havlicek (24) and Don Chaney (13) both serving as swingmen. A Havlicek injury prevented them from winning the playoffs.

Portland Trailblazers 1977. Won 60%. 5.5 Margin.

Their season record does not indicate their overall strength, when Bill Walton was injury-free. His 19-point average, coupled with Lucas' 20-point average, was augmented by Bob Gross, the defensive forward, and guards Lionel Hollins and low-scoring Dave Twardzik. Larry Steele and Herm Gilliam gave them good guards off the bench.

The Pairings

1. 1970 New York vs. 1972 Los Angeles
2. 1965 Boston vs. 1967 Philadelphia
3. 1972 Kentucky vs. 1973 Boston
4. 1971 Milwaukee vs. 1977 Portland

The All-Time Playoffs boast so much talent that anything could happen. Who will win may depend on such other factors as team depth or certain intangibles.

An overview of the eight finalists shows all but three teams—New York, and the two Boston teams—have centers who are powerful on both offense and defense. New York may make up for their center Willis Reed's less than dominating presence by being the best defensive team. Philadelphia is an offensive, Chamberlain-led machine, but may be outclassed by more balanced and more recent teams. Portland is weakened by Walton's penchant for getting injured. And here are three super winners: Los Angeles, which was offensive and fast-break oriented; Milwaukee, which slowed down for the high percentage shot and included the best shooters in this group; and Kentucky, which played both ways in compiling the ABA's best season ever. The first tipoff is at hand. Who do you pick to win the all-time title?

The Playoffs

First Round: 1972 Los Angeles vs. 1970 New York

The series promises to be a battle between the fast break offense of L.A. and the aggressive team defense of New York.

$$
\begin{array}{lccccc}
\text{LA} & 24 & 27 & 26 & 24 & 101 \\
\text{NY} & 21 & 22 & 20 & 18 & 81 \\
\end{array}
$$

In a tight defensive game, Los Angeles went up 51-43 at half and won going away. Frazier's 20, and Reed's and Debusschere's 14 each, could not hold up to the Lakers' balanced scoring, led by McMillan's 22.

$$
\begin{array}{lccccc}
\text{LA} & 36 & 23 & 28 & 35 & 122 \\
\text{NY} & 21 & 40 & 28 & 23 & 112 \\
\end{array}
$$

Down two going into the 4th quarter, the Lakers erupted for 35 points and the win. West's 49 point explosion and Goodrich's 22, overcame Frazier's 39 for N.Y.

$$
\begin{array}{lccccc}
\text{LA} & 25 & 33 & 27 & 35 & 120 \\
\text{NY} & 31 & 23 & 35 & 29 & 118 \\
\end{array}
$$

Trailing four as they began the fourth quarter, L.A. outbattled New York down the stretch to take a hard-fought 3-0 lead. Frazier's 43 and Reed's 32 fell two short of the more balanced attack of Los Angeles, which was led by West's 29 and McMillan's 23.

$$
\begin{array}{lccccc}
\text{LA} & 24 & 24 & 24 & 24 & 96 \\
\text{NY} & 21 & 21 & 18 & 21 & 81 \\
\end{array}
$$

Los Angeles won every quarter to clinch the series four games to none, in a repeat of the defensive struggle in game one. McMillan's 36 points and West's 22 offset Frazier's 27.

Chamberlain's rebounding dominated the series and the

Lakers' guards, West and Goodrich, simply outpointed the
high-scoring Frazier and the low-scoring Barnett.

First Round: 1967 Philadelphia vs. 1965 Boston

The Boston Celtic dynasty, which lost but one championship from 1959 through 1969, is matched against the inter-
lopers, who beat Boston in 1967.

Phil	23	35	31	36—125
Bos	28	17	20	23— 88

Sam Jones sparked Boston to an early fourteen point lead.
But Philadelphia was up by thirteen at the half and went on to
win handily. Greer's 30 and Jackson's 24 overcame Jones'
37.

Phil	34	31	23	37—125
Bos	21	12	28	26— 87

Jackson poured in 32 as the '76ers won going away.

Phil	36	18	40	35—129
Bos	23	26	27	25—101

Philly led 54-49 at half, but pulled away with Greer passing off for easy baskets and Cunningham scoring 19 in a
reserve role.

Phil	39	32	41	35—147
Bos	26	16	25	19— 86

The '76ers led 39-26 at the quarter, 71-42 at half, and
thoroughly demolished the demoralized Celtics. Greer had
49 for the winners. Philadelphia clinched the series four
games to none.

Philadelphia got a balanced attack from three forwards—Walker, Jackson and Cunningham, plus Chamberlain at center. Greer and K.C. Jones canceled each other

out at guard, but Boston could not get enough offense throughout their lineup to compete with the Sixers.

First Round: 1971 Milwaukee vs. 1977 Portland

In a battle of two former U.C.L.A. centers, Kareem Jabbar goes against Bill Walton in a private duel, while these patterned teams square off.

Mil	28	30	26	29—	113
Port	30	17	29	27—	103

Milwaukee pulled out to a 58-47 halftime lead and held on for the victory. Jabbar with 38 and Robertson with 32 topped Hollins with 24 and Lucas with 23. Gilliam had 13 off the bench for Portland.

Mil	31	24	26	31—	112
Port	35	34	18	22—	109

Portland led 69-55 at half. The team led by only six after the third quarter and were overtaken at the end. McGlocklin tied it with six minutes to go, and Robertson put in seven points at the end to claim the victory. Jabbar and Hollins each had 34. Walton had 19.

Mil	30	30	26	31—	117
Port	17	24	22	32—	95

On the strength of Jabbar, Milwaukee took an early 14-4 lead and gradually pulled away. Jabbar led all scorers with 43.

Mil	28	30	26	26—	110
Port	12	24	29	22—	87

Milwaukee got balanced scoring from McGlocklin, Robertson and Jabbar. The team took a 28-12 first quarter lead and then held on for the series, clinching the series, four games to none. Robertson had 35 and Jabbar 34. Portland was unable to get any offense going, save for Lucas' 20 points.

In the battle of two former UCLA centers, Walton won the rebounding, but Jabbar won the scoring with 38, 34, 43 and 34 point performances. Milwaukee's guards, Robertson and McGlocklin, outshone the up and down Hollins and the nonscoring Twardzik. Lucas had at least 20 points in each game, but Portland's offense was weak elsewhere.

First Round: 1972 Kentucky vs. 1973 Boston

This interleague battle matches the best single season team from the ABA versus a latter day version of the most successful NBA franchise, the Celtics.

Ky	19	34	35	29—117
Bos	22	22	24	33—101

Kentucky dominated the second quarter for a 53-44 lead at the half and never faltered. Issel's 34 and Gilmore's 30 led Kentucky. Havlicek had 42 and White 22 for Boston.

Ky	34	34	19	35—122
Bos	23	21	22	24— 90

Issel's 44 led the Colonels in a rout. They never trailed. Chaney had 30 in a losing cause.

Ky	29	35	35	34—133
Bos	33	24	24	22—103

As in game one, Kentucky wrapped up the contest in the second quarter with a 64-57 halftime lead that just kept growing. Gilmore had 46. Havlicek had 37, White 28, and Nelson 22 for Boston.

Ky	19	17	20	20—76
Bos	21	23	26	18—88

Silas, Nelson and White all scored over 20. Boston played

tremendous defense that stifled the Kentucky attack and won their first game.

Ky	19	35	28	36—118
Bos	22	24	34	23—103

Boston tried to duplicate the defensive strength they showed in game four, but trailed 54-46 at half and never quite caught up. Issel, Gilmore and Simon all scored over 20, while Nelson had 24 off the bench for Boston.

Without a big man to contain Gilmore, Boston was over-whelmed by the one-two punch of Issel and Gilmore. Boston's guards could not offset Kentucky's devastating front line, and lost the round four games to one.

Semifinal: 1972 Los Angeles vs. 1967 Philadelphia

It's Wilt vs. Wilt! Through the magic of computer game matchups, an ultimate fantasy happens here. The defensive Wilt of L.A. faces the scoring Chamberlain of Philadelphia.

LA	29	41	21	27—118
Phil	23	23	26	39—111

Goodrich's 12 and West's 9 points in quarter two put LA up 70-46 at half, and the team coasted to victory. Balanced scoring conquered Chamberlain's 31 and Walker's 24 points.

LA	40	21	42	29—132
Phil	22	26	20	27— 95

West's and Macmillan's 26 led a balanced attack that demolished Philly, even though Chamberlain had 33 and Greer 24 points for the losers.

LA	43	39	29	27—138
Phil	27	22	20	39—108

Los Angeles, with Goodrich's 28 points, led 82-46 at half, and held on for an easy third straight win.

```
LA     27   22   20   29— 98
Phil   39   25   27   23—114
```

Led by Chamberlain's 37 points, the '76ers played tight defense and broke a dry spell for their first win.

```
LA     21   29   29   25—104
Phil   26   23   41   37—127
```

The '76ers repeated their tight defensive performance; Chet Walker poured in 35 points, giving the team their second win and putting them back in contention.

```
LA     27   21   31   41—120
Phil   21   26   25   23— 95
```

Leading only 50-49 at half, the Lakers used McMillan's 28 points and Erickson's strong bench play to close out the series, clinching it four games to two.

Philadelphia was nearly a one man team, with Chamberlain scoring 30 or more in all but the last game. When Walker complemented his scoring and Philly played tight defense, they showed that Los Angeles could be beaten. However, a balanced attack by a devastating offensive machine was just too much L.A. for the '76ers to contain.

Semifinal: 1971 Milwaukee vs. 1973 Kentucky

Two pattern offenses, led by stars Jabbar and Robertson for the Bucks, versus Gilmore and Issel for the Colonels, promises a closely contested series.

```
Mil   25   16   22   30—93
Ky    22   19   33   20—94
```

Kentucky led by 11 going into the last quarter, yet almost blew it. Gilmore scored 34 and Issel 21, leading the Colonels in a squeaker.

```
Mil   29   26   31   33—117
Ky    18   32   37   22—109
```

Robertson went wild in the fourth quarter, feeding Jabbar and giving the Bucks the victory. Jabbar had 37, Robertson 28, and McGlocklin 22, overcoming Issel's 57.

Mil	26	28	33	27—114
Ky	28	42	22	24—116

Kentucky led by sixteen at half on the strength of 24 first half points by Issel. They held on, but barely, to take a 2-1 lead in games. Jabbar had 37 and Robertson 27 for the losing Bucks.

Mil	22	16	30	30—98
Ky	33	19	18	22—92

Kentucky faded again in the fourth quarter. Dandridge had 17, Jabbar 20, and Smith 22 as Milwaukee evened the series. Gilmore had 46 for the losers.

Mil	28	24	38	36—126
Ky	42	32	34	30—128

Kentucky led 74-52 at half and held on to take the series lead, three games to two. Issel poured in 57 for the winners.

Mil	25	30	17	15—87
Ky	22	20	19	19—80

Milwaukee led all the way in a tight defensive struggle. Jabbar's 12 points in the second quarter put the Colonels away and evened the series. Smith and Jabbar had 17, Robertson 16. Gilmore had 25, Issel 23, for the losers.

Mil	33	36	36	24—129
Ky	35	31	29	16—111

In a turnaround from the previous game, both teams played racehorse basketball. Milwaukee led 69-66 at the half and just kept pouring it on. The balanced scoring of Robertson with 38, Jabbar 33, and McGlocklin 24, won out over Gilmore's 34 and Issel's 21 for the Colonels.

Jabbar nullified Gilmore's usual height advantage and, although Issel was unstoppable for the Colonels, Milwaukee's overall team balance defeated Kentucky's one-two punch, four games to three.

Final: 1972 Los Angeles vs. 1971 Milwaukee

The All-Time Finals pitted two super teams, who actually competed against each other. Milwaukee won the 1971 NBA playoffs, but lost four games to two in the 1972 playoffs to the stronger Lakers. Now they meet, when they were both at their peaks.

```
LA    28   35   23   34—120
Mil   35   23   24   24—106
```

Los Angeles led by five at half and iced the game in the fourth quarter on 16 points by Goodrich. The big scorers were West 32, Goodrich 30, and Hairston 20 for the Lakers, while Robertson's 23, Jabbar's and McGlocklin's 21 each led the Bucks.

```
LA    30   26   37   21—114
Mil   31   39   23   24—117
```

Milwaukee led by 14 at half, were tied after three quarters, and pulled it out on ten fourth-quarter points by McGlocklin. Boozer scored 12, replacing the Bucks' Smith, who fouled out in quarter two. Dandridge was hurt and sat out the fourth quarter for Milwaukee.

```
LA    24   36   17   37—114
Mil   13   36   31   28—108
```

Los Angeles went from 11 up at half to three down after three quarters. Goodrich with 35 outshot Dandridge (22) down the stretch, giving the Lakers the win and a 2-1 edge in games.

```
LA    27   21   20   38—106
Mil   35   26   21   43—125
```

Milwaukee won every quarter to draw even for the series. Jabbar, Dandridge and Robertson all had 20 points for the winners.

LA	41	30	16	26—113
Mil	32	34	30	21—117

Milwaukee outscored Los Angeles by fourteen in the third quarter with balanced scoring, and held on to take the series lead 3-2. Jabbar had 27 and McGlocklin 29, to offset Goodrich's 40.

LA	16	21	42	37—116
Mil	33	24	28	28—113

Milwaukee was up 20 at half, and seemed to have the title in their grasp. But they were outscored by 14 in the third quarter and fell short at the end. West (31) and Goodrich (30) took over the game, while Boozer had 20 off the bench for the Bucks.

LA	28	39	24	36—127
Mil	32	37	26	29—124

Again Milwaukee led early, by two at half, and by four after three quarters. But the Lakers exploded for 36 in the last quarter. Led by Goodrich's bombs and West's foul shooting, Los Angeles won the all-time championship, four games to three.

In a very close series, the teams scored the same number of points, but Los Angeles won one more game. Although Milwaukee shot a better percentage, Chamberlain's stronger rebounding, and holding Jabbar in the 20's rather than his usual 30's, opened up the game for West and Goodrich. L.A.'s Hairston and McMillan were matched by Dandridge, Smith and Boozer at forward. Milwaukee got better scoring from their bench, but fell a little short to the Laker's explosive guards.

The 1972 Los Angeles Lakers reign as the all-time best in the history of basketball. In one year, this team collected all the elements of a superior team. The foundation was made of the old-timers, Wilt Chamberlain and Jerry West. Gail Goodrich complemented West at guard and became the leading scorer. Happy Hairston shared the rebounding with Chamberlain. McMillan replaced the aging Elgin Baylor as the scoring forward. Flynn Robinson and Pat Riley came off the bench with strength equal to the starters. All these elements were molded together by former player Bill Sharman, the new Los Angeles coach.

This team compiled the best season record in the history of the N.B.A. and won the championship playoffs. Now they have won the all-time playoffs. They stand as an example of greatness. They combined a former scorer, Chamberlain, who now played unselfishly; a team leader, West; and several young stars. They were not young enough to continue a dynasty, but for this one year, they were the best. Congratulations to some of the best players, and the best basketball team, of all-time.

The All-Time College Football Playoff

The Field

The All-Time College Football Playoff boasts some of the best coaches, players and teams in the sport's history. The final playoff came down to eight teams nationwide that had competed during the last twenty-five years. However, with the exception of Oklahoma of 1955, all teams competed in the last fifteen years. Obviously some local favorites did not make it, for these are the best of the best.

Of the teams competing, all were undefeated during the regular season, all went to bowls, and only Texas of 1977 lost. Some of the teams represent long winning streaks, such as Oklahoma's 47-game streak and Nebraska's 21-game run. Five of the groups won national titles, but all deserved them. All major conferences are represented, as well as two strong independents. All of the teams have powerful defenses, and all have great stars who later became pros. The coaches themselves represent a Hall of Fame. All that remains is to match them up and to see which emerges as the best of the best. Here is a preview of the eight finalists for the All-Time College Football Playoffs.

1955 Oklahoma Sooners (11-0) coach Bud Wilkinson

From the middle of college football's longest winning streak, 47 games in a row, come the split-T three plays-a-minute Sooners. They featured halfbacks Bob Burris and All-American junior Tommy McDonald, a line of Jerry Tubbs, Cecil Morris, Edmond Gray, Harold Burmine and All-American guard Bo Bollinger, with McDonald and Clendon Thomas offering great punt returns. They were a fabulous running team. They sailed through their season routing Nebraska 41-0, and became national champions by defeating undefeated, untied Maryland 20-6 in the Orange Bowl.

1966 Alabama Crimson Tide (11-0) coach Paul ''Bear'' Bryant

Boasting national championships in 1961, '64 and '65, Bryant called this #3 ranked team his best. With Kenny Stabler at quarterback leading a sprint-out attack and Ray Perkins and Dennis Homan catching passes, they were an exciting team to watch. They bested Tennessee 11-10 in late season and buried Nebraska in the Sugar Bowl.

1968 Ohio State Buckeyes (10-0) coach Woody Hayes

A brilliant, sophomore-laden team went undefeated, beat USC and O.J. Simpson in the Rose Bowl 27-16, and became national champs. Standouts were running and passing quarterback Rex Kern, runners, Leo Hayden and John Brockington, tight end Jan White, split end Bruce Jankowski, wingback Larry Zelina, cornerback Jack Tatum and defensive guard Jim Stillwagon. They lost but two games in three years.

1971 Nebraska Cornhuskers (13-0) coach Bob Devaney

This was their second consecutive national championship. In 1971, the Nebraska team outscored opponents 507-98, beat #2 ranked team, Oklahoma 35-31 at Norman in ''the battle of the century,'' and then another #2 ranked Alabama 38-6 in the Orange Bowl. Bear Bryant said, ''They might have been the greatest I've ever seen.'' Their spread-I slot-I was led by quarterback Jerry Tagge. Other offensive stars were I-back Jeff Kinney and All-American multi-talent Johnny Rodgers. On defense, middle guard Rich Glover, tackles Larry Jacobson and John Dutton, and end Willie Harper were all All-Americans.

1972 Southern California Trojans (12-0) coach John McKay

Playing a tough schedule, they beat Notre Dame 45-23,

UCLA 24-7 and #3 ranked Ohio State 42-17 in the Rose Bowl for the national title. Offensive stars were tight end Charles Young, Mike Rae and Pat Haden at quarterback, Sam "The Bam" Cunningham at fullback, wide receivers Lynn Swann and J.K. McKay, and Anthony Davis at tailback and break-away kick returner. Future All-Americans, linebacker Richard Wood and safety Artimus Parker, led the defense.

1973 Notre Dame Fighting Irish (11-0) coach Ara Parseghian

Winning their ninth national championship and preserving an eleventh perfect season, they survived close games with Michigan State and Southern California and beat Alabama 24-23 in a thriller in the Sugar Bowl. Quarterback Tom Clements led the Wing-T running attack, with halfbacks Eric Penick and Art Best and fullback Wayne Bullock. Other stars were guards Frank Pomarico and Gerry DiNardo and ends Dave Casper and Pete Demmerle. Safety Mike Townsend, end Ross Browner and tackle Mike Fanning led the defense, with Brian Doherty's punting and Bob Thomas' placements providing excellent kicking.

1973 Penn State Nittany Lions (12-0) coach Joe Paterno

The masters of the east, this team beat Pittsburgh and Tony Dorsett, 35-13, and then L.S.U. 16-9 in the Orange Bowl. Ranked only fifth, the pro-set team was led by Heisman winner John Cappelletti, quarterback Tom Shuman and place-kicker Chris Bahr. Defensive standouts were tackles Randy Crowder and Mike Hartenstine, end Dave Graf, and linebackers Chris Devlin and Greg Buttle.

1977 Texas Longhorns (11-1) coach Fred Akers

In a "rebuilding year," they ran up scores on Boston College (44-0), Virginia (68-0) and Rice (72-15). They upset Oklahoma, 13-6, and then were crushed 38-10 by Notre Dame in the Cotton Bowl. Stars were Heisman winner, Earl Campbell at running back; Outland Trophy winner, Brad Shearer, at defensive tackle; kicker Russell Erxleben, who set an NCAA field goal record with a 67 yarder; quarterback Randy McEachern; and receivers Alfred Jackson and Lam Jones.

The Pairings

1971 Nebraska vs. 1977 Texas
1973 Notre Dame vs. 1966 Alabama
1973 Penn State vs. 1955 Oklahoma
1968 Ohio State vs. 1972 Southern California

The All-Time College Football playoff is dominated by five teams from the 1970's. One big question to be answered is whether the three teams from the 1950's and 1960's can compete with them.

Four teams in the field possess wide-open running attacks. Nebraska, Texas, Oklahoma and Southern California can score almost at will by the run. Will the sprint-out passing of Alabama or the more balanced attack of Notre Dame, Penn State and Ohio State be a handicap or a disadvantage against the explosive running teams?

One interesting feature of this playoff is that three of the teams, Notre Dame, Penn State and Ohio State, sent an unusual number of players to the pros. Their style of play, not being quite as wide-open and perhaps more defensive-minded, presents a contrast to most of the teams. Will the pro style win in the college game? That is, perhaps, the central question.

We're ready for the opening kickoff. Who is your pick as college football's All-Time Best?

The Playoffs

First Round: Nebraska 1971 vs. Texas 1977

Two offensive machines, led by Johnny Rodgers' big plays for Nebraska and Earl Campbell's steadiness for Texas, promises a wild scorning game.

Nebraska	7	0	14	13—34
Texas	2	0	0	7— 9

Scoring

Rodgers (N) 26 yd TD run, Sanger conversion.
Shearer (T) tackled Kinney (N) for safety.
Tagge (N) 2 yd TD run, Sanger conversion.
Kinney (N) 13 yd TD run, Sanger conversion.
Campbell (T) 2 yd TD run, Erxleben conversion.
Rodgers (N) 18 yd TD pass from Tagge, conversion failed.
Blahak (N) 94 yd TD interception return, Sanger conversion.

Nebraska blocked a Longhorn punt during the first series of the game and took over on their 41. Three plays later, Johnny Rodgers ran 26 yards for a score that started the Nebraska romp. On their next possession, Nebraska back Jeff Kinney was tackled by defensive tackle Brad Shearer for a safety. Both teams had several drives fizzle, and it remained 7 to 2 at the half.

In the third quarter, Nebraska scored twice. One score was from two yards by quarterback Jerry Tagge, on a 31-yard march after a 53-yard interception return. Later, Rodgers returned a punt 72 yards to the Texas 13, and Kinney ran it in. Texas marched 72 yards, with Earl Campbell scoring from the two as the fourth quarter began. At that point it was 21 to 9. Late in the game, a Texas fumble on their own 18 set the stage for an eighteen-yard touchdown run by Rodgers. The last score came on a pass, which was picked off by Blahak at the Nebraska six and returned 94 yards for a score. The opportunistic Cornhuskers buried Texas 34-9.

Texas 1977		Nebraska 1971
16	1st Downs	14
41-21	Rushing	32-105
39-25-5:236	Passing	25-18-1:120
8-166	Returns	7-252
6-208	Punts	6-228
3-25	Penalties Against	2-28
2-1	Fumbles, Lost	0

First Round: Notre Dame 1973 vs. Alabama 1966

A sound all-around Irish team is matched against Ken Stabler's sprint-out passing game.

Notre Dame	0	14	14	14—42
Alabama	0	7	0	7—14

Scoring

Stabler (A) 1 yd TD run, Davis conversion.

Demmerle (ND) 4 yd TD pass from Clements, Thomas conversion.

Casper (ND) 7 yd TD pass from Clements, Thomas conversion.

Clements (ND) 3 yd TD run, Thomas conversion.

Bullock (ND) 5 yd TD pass from Clements, Thomas conversion.

Demmerle (ND) 3 yd TD pass from Clements, Thomas conversion.

Townsend (ND) 21 yd TD interception return, Thomas conversion.

Perkins (A) 6 yd TD pass from Stabler, Davis conversion.

With 2:20 left in the first half, Alabama had throttled the Irish at every turn, holding them to one first down while maintaining a 7-0 lead. Then the roof fell in! On a first down from their own 10, Stabler fumbled, and two plays later, Clements hit Demmerle for a touchdown. It was 7-7. After the kickoff, Alabama fumbled again on their own 15. Again Clements threw a scoring pass, this time to Casper, and it was 14-7 at half.

Without the fumbles, Alabama had looked slightly better in the first half, while Notre Dame had shown no offense. The Irish changed all that. With two long marches in the third quarter, they took a 28-7 lead. From then on, the game deteriorated, as Stabler threw four desperation interceptions. Stabler tacked on a scoring pass to Perkins to end the scoring.

Two fumbles and two scoring drives had told the story.

Notre Dame 1973		Alabama 1966
15	1st Downs	18
38-90	Rushing	36-76
26-25-0:198	Passing	35-19-5:189
10-102	Returns	4-66
7-276	Punts	4-146
10-65	Penalties Against	0
3-3	Fumbles, Lost	4-3

First Round: Penn State 1973 vs. Oklahoma 1955

The best Penn State team boasts a pro-set offense and goes against the powerful running attack of the Sooners, which gave them 47 straight wins.

Penn State	7	17	0	14—38
Oklahoma	12	6	0	8—26

Scoring

McDonald (O), 28 yd TD run, conversion failed.
Burris (O), 8 yd TD run, 2 pt. conversion failed.
Hayman (PS), 4 yd TD pass from Shuman, Bahr conversion.
McDonald (O), 2 yd TD run, 2 pt. conversion failed.
Cappelletti (PS), 9 yd TD run, Bahr conversion.
Cappelletti (PS), 13 yd TD run, Bahr conversion.
Bahr (PS), 35 yd field goal.
Cappelletti (PS), 37 yd TD run, Bahr conversion.
Nagle (PS) 11 yd TD run, Bahr conversion.
McDonald (O), 12 yd TD pass, McDonald 2 pt. conversion.

Oklahoma chose to receive the opening kickoff and marched down the field for a touchdown, which was capped by Tommy McDonald's 28-yard scamper. On Penn State's first play from scrimmage, the handoff was fumbled at their own 19. Four plays later, Burris went eight yards on a counter for a 12-0 Oklahoma lead. Tom Shuman then mixed passing and Cappelletti's running for three straight touchdowns and a Penn State lead that held for the game. Oklahoma scored again, but fumbled at their own 29 near halftime. Bahr added a field goal for a 24-18 halftime Penn State lead.

The third quarter was scoreless, but Penn State broke some long gainers for a 38-18 lead early in the fourth. Oklahoma marched 79 yards and scored on the last play of the game to gain a little respectability.

Penn State 1973		Oklahoma 1955
18	1st Downs	17
51-310	Rushing	60-317
8-4-0:50	Passing	8-3-0:28
6-152	Returns	6-125
4-150	Punts	6-245
7-65	Penalties Against	8-85
1-1	Fumbles, Lost	2-1

First Round: Ohio State 1968 vs. Southern California 1972

Two talent-laden teams feature John Brockington's plunges for the deliberate Buckeyes against Anthony Davis' big plays and long kickoff returns for the Trojans.

Ohio State	0	0	0	14—14
U.S.C.	0	7	0	3—10

Scoring

Davis (SC), 39 yd TD run, Rae conversion.
Brockington (O), 1 yd TD run, Roman conversion.
Rae (SC), 16 yd field goal.
White (O), 2 yd TD pass from Kern, Roman conversion.

After a half marred by several turnovers, Southern California returned an interception to the Ohio State 44 with thirty seconds left. On the last play of the half, Anthony Davis scampered 39 yards for a score, and the Trojans led 7-0.

Early in the fourth quarter, the Buckeyes marched 76 yards with Brockington going over from the one for a 7-7 tie. After a short kickoff, which was returned to the State 34, Davis broke loose to set up Rae's go-ahead field goal. The Buckeyes then marched 86 yards on the running of Hayden and Brockington, and completed a final two-yard scoring pass from Rex Kern to Jan White. State led for the first time 14-10. Davis returned the kickoff to the 34, and then broke loose for 33 yards to the Buckeye 33. However, a 15-yard penalty and an interception of a Pat Hayden pass, sealed the victory for Woody Hayes' Buckeyes in a very tight game.

Ohio State 1968		Southern California 1972
16	1st Downs	15
46-241	Rushing	59-221
24-14-2:41	Passing	9-2-2:53
5-37	Returns	6-108
7-240	Punts	6-218
10-101	Penalties Against	7-82
1-0	Fumbles, Lost	3-2

Semifinal: Penn State 1973 vs. Nebraska 1971

The pro-type offense and defense of the Nittany Lions is matched against the wide-open offense of Nebraska.

Penn State	3	21	7	21—52
Nebraska	0	7	0	0— 7

Scoring

Bahr (PS), 35 yd field goal.
Bradley (PS), 81 yd TD punt return, Bahr conversion.
Scott (PS), 48 yd TD pass from Shuman, Bahr conversion.
Cappelletti (PS), 15 yd TD run, Bahr conversion.
Rodgers (N), 6 yd TD run, Sanger conversion.

Shuman (PS), 2 yd TD run, Bahr conversion.
Cappelletti (PS), 8 yd TD run, Bahr conversion.
Nagle (PS), 2 yd TD run, Bahr conversion.
Cappelletti (PS), 5 yd TD run, Bahr conversion.

Penn State sported a 3-0 lead. But, after a Chris Bahr field goal in the first quarter, Bradley returned a punt 81 yards for a touchdown and Penn State's lead stretched to 10-0. From then on, the floodgates were open. Shuman threw 48 yards to Scott for one touchdown. Cappelletti ran fifteen for another. Rodgers took the kickoff back to the Penn State 6 and scored two plays later, giving Nebraska its only score. It was 24-7 at half.

Penn State put together four long, time-consuming drives in the second half. Shuman ran in on a two-yard rollout. Cappelletti went eight yards on a counter. Nagle went two yards off-tackle. Finally, Cappelletti ran for a five-yard score. The contest ended 52-7. Nebraska was never in the game.

Penn State 1973		Nebraska 1971
21	1st Downs	11
52-336	Rushing	32-120
16-10-1:139	Passing	29-17-0:147
6-164	Returns	8-245
5-166	Punts	9-313
5-45	Penalties Against	8-76
2-0	Fumbles, Lost	6-3

Semifinal: Notre Dame 1973 vs. Ohio State 1968

Notre Dame showed more offense in their first round game, while the Buckeyes won a low-scoring defensive struggle.

Notre Dame	0	12	7	10—	29
Ohio State	7	0	0	0—	7

Scoring

Hayden (O), 11 yd TD run, Roman conversion.

Casper (ND), 5 yd TD pass from Clements, conversion failed.

Best (ND), 9 yd TD run, conversion failed.

Penick (ND), 10 yd TD run, Bullock 2 pt. conversion (run).

Thomas (ND), 23 yd field goal.

Best (ND), 10 yd TD run, Thomas conversion.

Late in the first quarter, Notre Dame fumbled on their own eleven. On the next play, Leo Hayden ran eleven yards for an Ohio State score and a 7-0 lead. It was their last hurrah. Notre Dame marched 77 yards, scoring on a Clements to Casper pass. Missing the extra point, Notre Dame trailed 7-6 with 1:20 left in the half. The Buckeyes fumbled the kickoff at their own 3, and punted from the 4. Townsend returned the punt to the Buckeye 17. A piling on penalty put it on the nine, and Best ran it on the last play of the half. The point was missed and the Irish led 12-7. In the third quarter, the Irish ran a short punt back to the Buckeye 32. Five plays later, Penick ran ten yards and the score was 19 to 7. Thomas added a field goal and Best ran ten yards for the final score. Notre Dame won three of the quarters, besting the Buckeyes 29 to 7.

Notre Dame 1973		Ohio State 1968
13	1st Downs	14
52-205	Rushing	48-212
7-7-0:34	Passing	21-10-3:40
7-101	Returns	3-14
7-289	Punts	7-234
6-63	Penalties Against	3-30
3-3	Fumbles, Lost	2-1

Final: Penn State 1973 vs. Notre Dame 1973

Two powerhouse independents from the same year of college football squared off. This game was prevented in

1973, when they went to different bowls. The teams showed
plenty of offense in their two previous playoff games. If Penn
State had indicated any weakness, it was in allowing Oklahoma to rush for four touchdowns. Notre Dame's weakness
seemed to be a tendency to fall behind early in their games.

The stage is set for the All-Time Championship.

Penn State	7	7	8	6—28
Notre Dame	0	8	22	14—44

Scoring

Cappelletti (PS), 12 yd TD run, Bahr conversion.

Nagle (PS), 14 yd TD pass from Shuman, Bahr conversion.

Penick (ND), 2 yd TD pass from Clements, Best 2 pt.
conversion.

Clements (ND), 6 yd TD run, Penick 2 pt. conversion.

Casper (ND), 12 yd TD pass from Clements, conversion
failed.

Best (ND), 1 yd TD pass from Clements, Penick 2 pt.
conversion.

Bullock (ND), 3 yd TD pass from Clements, Best 2 pt.
conversion.

Demmerle (ND), 11 yd TD pass from Clements, Bullock 2
pt. conversion.

Hayman (PS), 84 yd TD kickoff return, conversion failed.

Following the pattern of their two previous games, Notre
Dame fell behind early, then gathered momentum, and
buried their opponent. In mid-first quarter, State returned a
short punt to the Irish 24 and, two plays later, Cappelletti
went twelve yards for the score. State later started an 80-yard
drive that carried into the second quarter and gave them a
14-0 lead. Notre Dame went 69 yards in five plays, scoring
on the last play of the half. A two-yard Clements to Penick
pass made it 14-8.

The Irish returned the second half kickoff 74 yards and
went on to score in their next four possessions. Clements ran

in one, and passed to Casper, Best, and Bullock for scores to put the game out of reach, 38-22. Capelletti ran in a touchdown for State.

In the fourth quarter, each team added another score. Notre Dame scored on a pass to Demmerle, and State on an 84-yard kickoff return by Hayman. It ended up 44-28 for Notre Dame.

The two independents from the same year had put on a powerful offensive show, with the Irish emerging as the more powerful.

Penn State 1973		Notre Dame 1973
21	1st Downs	25
59-323	Rushing	25-103
6-3-0:48	Passing	44-25-1:344
6-192	Returns	6-189
4-149	Punts	3-120
8-77	Penalties Against	6-42
5-0	Fumbles, Lost	3-3

Notre Dame rests on the tradition of Knute Rockne and Frank Leahy, George Gipp and the Four Horsemen. The first dynasty under Rockne had a record of 105-12-5 during 1918-30. Leahy's record for the second dynasty was 97-11-9, 1941-54. From 1887-1958 the Irish had only five losing seasons. From 1959 to 1963 the Irish had five losing seasons and called on Ara Parseghian to rescue them. He started their third dynasty in 1964. During the next ten years they missed the top ten only once and ranked first in 1966 and 1973.

Undoubtedly the historic glamour team of college football, with a fight song that has made them known to all, Notre Dame still has the number one all-time winning percentage.

It is no accident then that Notre Dame emerged as the All-time champs. Our salute goes to Ara Parseghian and all the great players that made the 1973 Notre Dame Fighting Irish the greatest of all-time. They are the best in a long line of greats linking that great football tradition.

The All-Time Pro Football Playoff

The Field

Professional football has a rich history which dates back to the 1920's and includes names such as Jim Thorpe and Red Grange. It developed from a running game to a passing game under Sammy Baugh in the 1940's. Great teams from its earlier years were the Chicago Bears, Washington Redskins, Detroit Lions, Cleveland Browns and Green Bay Packers. However, it is with the Green Bay Packers of the 1960's that the league reached the level of sophistication of this all-time championship.

Following the 1965 season, two rival leagues joined to form the National Football League, retaining National and American conferences that would meet in a Super Bowl. For this all-time playoff, six of the eight teams come from the Super Bowl Era. Only the Baltimore Colts of 1958 and the Green Bay Packers of 1962 qualified to compete with the great teams of the later Super Bowl years. Here is a preview of the eight teams who will compete for the all-time title, in what has become the number one sport in the United States:

1958 Baltimore Colts. Winning nine and losing three during the season, this Weeb Eubank coached team beat New York 23-17 in overtime for the championship, and repeated the next year. They were led by Johnny Unitas at quarterback, who threw 19 touchdown passes. Ray Berry with 56 receptions and Lenny Moore with 50 did the catching, while Alan Ameche led the running attack with a 4.6 average. Jim Parker at offensive tackle, and Gino Marchetti and Big Daddy Lipscomb on defense were standouts.

1962 Green Bay Packers. They had a 13-1 season and beat New York 16-7 in the championship. Vince Lombardi's teams won five titles between 1961 and 1967. This was the best year of the Packer Dynasty, a year in which Bart Starr, at quarterback, completed an amazing 62 percent of his passes to receivers Max McGee, Boyd Dowler, and Ron Kramer. Fullback Jim Taylor, with a 5.4 average, led the running attack. Loaded with stars, the team also possessed an unusually strong pass defense.

1969 Kansas City Chiefs. They were 11-3 for the season, 3-0 for the playoffs, and beat Minnesota 23-7 in Super Bowl IV. Hank Stram's squad lost twice to Oakland during the season, but beat them in the playoffs. They went on to win the Super Bowl to become the second AFL winner. Len Dawson and Mike Livingston shared the passing. Mike Garrett, Robert Holmes, and Warren McVea keyed their diverse running attack. Otis Taylor led a group of five receivers with twenty or more receptions. The team boasted three strong linebackers in Bobby Bell, Willie Lanier and Jim Lynch. They pioneered the "I Offense" to hide the backs from the defense.

1969 Minnesota Vikings. Going 12-2 for the season, they won two playoff games before losing the Super Bowl to the Kansas City Chiefs. Bud Grant's team was led by the average passing but mad, scrambling running of quarterback Joe Kapp. Chief runners were Dave Osborn and Bill Brown, while Gene Washington caught 39 passes to lead the team. But the Viking strength was defense. The Front Four consisting of Carl Eller, Jim Marshall, Gary Larsen and Alan Page, also known as the "Purple People Eaters," gave the Vikings the ball constantly, making offense almost an afterthought.

1973 Miami Dolphins. They were 12-2 during the season, swept three straight in the playoffs, and beat Minnesota 24-7 in the Super Bowl. Don Shula's team from the previous year had an NFL record, 17-0 season. However, this team was slightly better, containing a healthy Bob Griese at quarter-back for the entire season. Oakland broke their win streak at nineteen in early season. Their other loss was to Baltimore, while Griese was rested. Larry Csonka (4.6) and Mercury Morris (6.4) ran, while Marlin Briscoe and Paul Warfield caught passes sparingly when they were needed. The "no name" defense kept others contained, but ball control was their strength.

1973 Oakland Raiders. This great team was only 9-4-1 in the season and 1-1 in the playoffs, bowing to Miami 10-27. How can a team with five losses be among the eight best of all-time? Would not the Oakland team of 1976, which won the Super Bowl, be a better entry? A certain amount of luck is involved and this team had little. After three games and no touchdowns, Ken Stabler and short passing replaced Daryl Lamonica and long passing at quarterback for coach John Madden. Marv Hubbard (4.7), Charlie Smith (3.9), and Clarence Davis (5.3) ran, and Fred Biletnikoff and Mike Siani caught passes. Penalties and fumbles keyed their play-off loss to Miami. However, this is the team that stopped Miami's unbeaten string, 12-7, in the third game of the season and were the only ones in Miami's class that year.

1974 Pittsburgh Steelers. They had a 10-3 season and went 3-0 in the playoffs, beating Minnesota 16-6 in the Super Bowl. Chuck Noll's team combined a devastating defense with the ball control of Franco Harris' running. They took the championship and repeated the next year. Joe Gilliam and Terry Bradshaw shared the quarterbacking, passing to chief receiver Frank Lewis. But the running of Harris (4.8), backed by Rocky Blier (4.2), was the offense.

1977 Dallas Cowboys. Their season was 12-2, included a 3-0 playoff, and was topped by a 27-10 defeat of Denver in the Super Bowl. Tom Landry's offensive machine was led by Roger Staubach's passing, Tony Dorsett's running (4.8), and the receiving of Dorsett and Preston Pearson. They gave the

national conference its first title since Dallas won in 1971. In
beating Minnesota and Denver twice each, Dallas proved
they were the class of a balanced league.

The Pairings

1969 Minnesota vs. 1973 Miami
1969 Kansas City vs. 1977 Dallas
1973 Oakland vs. 1974 Pittsburgh
1958 Baltimore vs. 1962 Green Bay

The All-Time Pro Football Playoffs feature teams from
some of the great dynasties of recent NFL history. The
Miami, Dallas, and Pittsburgh franchises now have compiled
records that rival the Lombardi years at Green Bay. The
Green Bay Packers of 1962 often have been considered the
best pro football team of all-time. However, in this playoff
they are outnumbered by more modern teams. Will Green
Bay hold up under the challenge of the new style of the late
sixties and seventies? Green Bay's fourteen wins and one
loss was a record performance, but Miami of 1972 broke that
mark with a perfect 17-0 season. Ironically, that record-
breaking Miami team of 1972 was judged less effective than
the Dolphins of the following year. Will Miami, or another
modern team, highlight weaknesses in the great Green Bay
team?

Since the beginning of the Super Bowl, only three teams
have been repeat winners. The 1967-68 winners, Green Bay,
are not represented in this playoff. The other two teams,
Miami of 1972-73 and Pittsburgh of 1974-75, are competing
for the all-time title. With the exception of Minnesota, all the
other franchises represented here have won at least one Super
Bowl. However, the two oldest teams, Green Bay of 1962
and Baltimore of 1958, won titles before the advent of the
Super Bowl. If total Super Bowl wins were important in
deciding the all-time champs, then Pittsburgh—with four
non-consecutive wins—should be considered slight favo-

rites. However, if total championships were counted and included those before the Super Bowl's appearance, then Green Bay would be a prohibitive favorite. They won five yearly championships between 1961 and 1967.

The Packers, Dolphins, and Steelers have a strong tradition for winning, which should make them slight favorites for the playoffs. Most of the eight teams have standout quarterbacks and excellent defenses. Green Bay with Taylor, Miami with Csonka, and Pittsburgh with Harris seem to have the best running attacks. The eventual winner might be the team which can make the others play their type of game. This seems particularly true of Pittsburgh and Miami, who require ball control to make their teams go. And the question remains: Can Green Bay play with the moderns? As the playoffs begin, who do you pick as the all-time best?

The Playoffs

First Round: 1973 Miami vs. 1969 Minnesota

The contest shaped up as a struggle between Miami's running game and Minnesota's feared front four in the defensive line.

The teams traded field goals in the first quarter, but Minnesota went up 6-3 early in the second quarter on a second field goal. Just before the half ended, the Dolphins put together a drive that was capped by a Larry Csonka plunge for the touchdown, resulting in a 10-6 lead.

The Vikings fumbled on their first possession of the second half. On the next play, Bob Griese threw 33 yards to Paul Warfield for a score, and the Dolphins led 17 to 6. Minnesota came back throwing, scoring on a 25-yard pass from Joe Kapp to Gene Washington. Yet the northern team still trailed 17 to 13. Miami put together another long march, with Csonka going over from the three, to make it 24-13.

Minnesota got the only score in the fourth quarter on a

two-yard run by Dave Osborn, which cut the lead to 24-20.
Miami played ball control to hold onto the victory.

Errorless play and Csonka's 131 yards rushing made the
difference in this matchup.

```
              1973 Miami        3   7  14   0—24
              1969 Minnesota    3   3   7   7—20
```

1st Q	Miami	Yepremian 22 yd field goal
	Minn.	Cox 29 yd field goal
2nd Q	Minn.	Cox 19 yd field goal
	Miami	Csonka 2 yd TD rush, PAT—Yepremian (kick)
3rd Q	Miami	Warfield 33 yd TD pass from Griese, PAT—Cox (kick)
	Minn.	Washington 25 yd TD pass from Kapp, PAT—Cox (kick)
	Miami	Csonka 3 yd TD rush, PAT—Yepremian (kick)
4th Q	Minn.	Osborn 2 yd TD rush, PAT—Cox (kick)

Miami		*Minnesota*
21	1st Downs	16
53-231	Rushing	32-144
5-58	Passing	12-184
83	Returns	70
5-7-0	Passes	12-21-2
2-39.0	Punts	3-35.0
1-0	Fumbles, Lost	3-2
2-15	Penalties—Yards	4-36

Rushing—Csonka 31 for 131 yards, Morris 13 for 60 yards,
Kiick 6 for 11 yards, Griese 2 for 23 yards, Nottingham
1 for 6 yards; Osborn 13 for 62 yards, Brown 9 for 35
yards, Reed 5 for 12 yards, Kapp 5 for 35 yards.

Passing—Griese 5 of 7 for 58 yards. Kapp 12 of 21 for 184
yards, 2 intercepted.

Receiving—Warfield 2 for 40 yards, Briscoe 2 for 16 yards,
Kiick 1 for 2 yards; Henderson 5 for 64 yards, Washing-

ton 2 for 65 yards, Brown 2 for 16 yards, Beasley 2 for 36 yards, Reed 1 for 3 yards.

First Round: 1977 Dallas vs. 1969 Kansas City

Two of the most spectacular offensive attacks were matched for a real free-for-all in this game.

Len Dawson found Otis Taylor open and hit him for a 33-yard touchdown strike in the first quarter. Dallas put together running and passing and Dorsett ran four yards to tie it as the second quarter started. Kansas City put together a short drive, but settled for a Jan Stenerud field goal to go up 10-7. Roger Staubach got his passes clicking late in the half. Drew Pearson caught one at the ten and skipped in for a 14-10 half time lead.

Both teams fizzled in the third quarter, until Herrera hit a field goal for a 17-10 lead. In the fourth quarter, Staubach sneaked in from two yards to put the Cowboys up 24-10. Kansas City came back on a plunge by Garrett, but it was too late. Dallas won the offensive show 24-17.

1977 Dallas		0	14	3	7	24
1969 Kansas City	7	3	0	7	17

1st Q	KC	Taylor, 33 yd TD pass from Dawson, PAT—Stenerud (kick)
2nd Q	Dall	Dorsett, 4 yd TD rush, PAT—Herrera (kick)
	KC	Stenerud, 31 yd field goal
	Dall	D. Pearson, 21 yd TD pass from Staubach, PAT—Herrera (kick)
3rd Q	Dall	Herrera, 27 yd field goal
4th Q	Dall	Staubach, 2 yd TD rush, PAT—Herrera (kick)
	KC	Garrett, 3 yd TD rush, PAT—Stenerud (kick)

Dallas		*Kansas City*
17	1st Downs	15
39-74	Rushing	39-119
15-174	Passing	7-105
72	Returns	75
24-15-1	Passes	17-7-1
6-39.1	Punts	6-45.7
4-2	Fumbles, Lost	3-2
7-72	Penalties—Yards	5-45

Rushing—Dorsett 17 for 68 yards, Newhouse 15 for 68 yards, Staubach 3 for 5 yards, P. Pearson 3 for 19 yards, D. White 1 for 14 yards; Holmes 12 for 11 yards, Garrett 9 for 29 yards, Hayes 8 for 33 yards, McVea 8 for 20 yards, Pitts 2 for 26 yards.

Passing—Staubach 15 for 24 for 174 yards, one intercepted. Dawson 7 for 17 for 105 yards, one intercepted.

Receiving—P. Pearson 4 for 43 yards, DuPree 3 for 47 yards, D. Pearson 3 for 46 yards, Richards 2 for 36 yards, Newhouse 3 for 2 yards; Taylor 4 for 72 yards, Pitts 2 for 27 yards, Holmes 1 for 6 yards.

First Round: 1973 Oakland vs. 1974 Pittsburgh

Two strong teams from the American Football Conference met to bump heads in an expected defensive duel. In 1973 and 1974 they split two meetings.

Defense held strong for the first two possessions on each side. Then, late in the first quarter, Ken Stabler mixed short passes and runs for a 61-yard drive. Marv Hubbard went over from the three and George Blanda's kick made it 7-0. Pittsburgh came back by way of the run. Franco Harris scored from the five, and Roy Gerela made it 7-7. Stabler hurried a drive on sideline passes, and, with fifty seconds in the half, Blanda kicked a 24 yard field goal for a 10-7 halftime lead.

In a defensive third quarter, Gerela got a 30-yard field goal for the Steelers to tie it 10-10. Midway through the fourth quarter, Stabler fashioned a drive that ended with a 17-yard touchdown pass to Siani. Oakland held on to win. Stabler's

pinpoint passing overcame Franco Harris' 123 yards rushing
and gave Oakland the victory.

1973 Oakland	7	3	0	7—17
1974 Pittsburgh	0	7	3	0—10

1st Q	Oak	Hubbard, 3-yd TD rush, PAT—Blanda
2nd Q	Pitt	Harris, 5-yd TD rush, PAT—Gerela
	Oak	Blanda, 24-yd field goal
3rd Q	Pitt	Gerela, 30-yd field goal
4th Q	Oak	Siani, 17-yd TD pass from Stabler; PAT—Blanda

Oakland		Pittsburgh
20	1st Downs	11
35-143	Rushing	38-166
20-172	Passing	6-64
119	Returns	68
31-20-1	Passes	10-6-0
5-51.0	Punts	7-34.7
1-0	Fumbles, Lost	4-2
4-47	Penalties—Yards	6-81

Rushing—Hubbard 13 for 72 yards, C. Smith 13 for 47
yards, C. Davis 6 for 20 yards, Banaszak 3 for 4 yards;
Harris 23 for 123 yards, Bleier 12 for 43 yards, Bradshaw 3 for 0 yards.

Passing—Stabler 20 for 31 for 172 yards, one interception,
Bradshaw 6 for 10 for 64 yards.

Receiving—C. Smith 7 for 57 yards, Siani 4 for 60 yards,
Biletnikoff 3 for 20 yards, Hubbard 3 for 18 yards,
Moore 3 for 17 yards; Brown 2 for 33 yards, Bleier 1 for
5 yards, Swann 1 for 10 yards, Stallworth 2 for 16
yards.

First Round: 1958 Baltimore vs. 1962 Green Bay

The two oldest teams in the playoffs have strong defenses
and outstanding quarterbacks in Johnny Unitas and Bart
Starr. The edge, if any, is probably in Green Bay's running
attack.

Green Bay scored on their first possession, marching to the

19, where Starr threw to Max McGee for a 7-0 lead. Baltimore came back with a Steve Myhra field goal to make it 7-3. In the second quarter, the Packers put the game away with touchdowns by Jim Taylor or on a four-yard run, and a 13-yard Starr to Ron Kramer pass.

Trailing 21-3 at half, Baltimore put together a third quarter drive that saw Alan Ameche go over from the three. That push ended the Colts' game. Taylor plunged over from the two and Jim Kramer added a fourth quarter field goal for the 31-10 win.

Run or pass, Green Bay could not be stopped. Their defense blunted Unitas' passing game and they won impressively.

1962 Green Bay	7	14	7	3—31
1958 Baltimore	3	0	7	0—10

1st Q	GB	McGee, 19 yd TD pass from Starr, PAT—J. Kramer (kick)
	Balt	Myhra, 15 yd field goal
2nd Q	GB	Taylor, 4 yd TD rush, PAT—J. Kramer (kick)
	GB	R. Kramer 13 yd TD pass from Starr, PAT—J. Kramer (kick)
3rd Q	Balt	Ameche, 3 yd TD rush, PAT—Myhra (kick)
	GB	Taylor, 2 yd TD rush, PAT—J. Kramer (kick)
4th Q	GB	J. Kramer, 25 yd field goal

Green Bay		Baltimore
24	1st Downs	14
36-146	Rushing	26-93
20-213	Passing	13-180
83	Returns	138
20-34-0	Passes	13-26-1
3-36.0	Punts	6-50.8
2-0	Fumbles, Lost	2-2
5-44	Penalties—Yards	3-15

Rushing—Taylor 24 for 95 yards, Hornung 6 for 24 yards, Moore 5 for 21 yards, Starr 1 for 6 yards; Ameche 10 for 40 yards, Dupre 8 for 20 yards, Unitas 3 for 19 yards, Moore 5 for 14 yards.

Passing—Starr 19 for 33 for 194 yards, Hornung 1 for 1 for 21 yards. Unitas 13 for 26 for 180 yards, 1 interception.

Receiving—Dowler 7 for 84 yards, Taylor 5 for 34 yards, R. Kramer 4 for 50 yards, McGee 4 for 45 yards; Berry 6 for 83 yards, Moore 3 for 58 yards, Mutscheller 2 for 32 yards, Ameche 1 for 5 yards, Dupre 1 for 2 yards.

Semifinal: 1973 Miami vs. 1977 Dallas

Miami's defense was matched against the exciting Dallas offense in this first semifinal game.

Miami scored the first two times they had the ball. Larry Csonka capped a 79-yard march with a four-yard run. A little later, Jim Kiick went over from the two for a 14-0 lead. Dallas, forced to play catch-up, got a second quarter score on a Roger Staubach pass to Preston Pearson. Miami added another touchdown on a five-yard Csonka run, and a 24-yard field goal by Garo Yepremian to go up 24-7 at half.

In the third quarter, Staubach threw six yards to Dorsett for a score. Miami came back on a 15-yard touchdown run by Mercury Morris. Herrera got a 33-yard field goal for the Cowboys. Trailing 31-17, Dallas failed on an onside kick attempt. Miami played ball control in the fourth quarter and put the game away with a time-consuming drive. Csonka scored his third touchdown from the two, and the Dolphins looked strong, winning 38-17.

1973 Miami	14	10	7	7—38
1977 Dallas	0	7	10	0—17

1st Q	Miami	Csonka, 4 yd TD rush, PAT—Yepremian (kick)
	Miami	Kiick, 2 yd TD rush, PAT—Yepremian (kick)

2nd Q	Dall	P. Pearson, 13 yd TD pass from Staubach, PAT—Herrera (kick)
	Miami	Csonka, 5 yd TD rush, PAT—Yepremian (kick)
	Miami	Yepremian, 24 yd field goal
3rd Q	Dall	Dorsett, 6 yd TD pass from Staubach, PAT—Herrera (kick)
	Miami	Morris, 15 yd TD rush, PAT—Yepremian (kick)
	Dall	Herrera, 33 yd field goal
4th Q	Miami	Csonka, 2 yd TD rush, PAT—Yepremian (kick)

Miami		*Dallas*
27	1st Downs	11
52-241	Rushing	26-113
11-159	Passing	12-158
20	Returns	125
18-11-1	Passes	23-12-1
2-49.0	Punts	6-34.7
2-1	Fumbles, Lost	1-1
1-5	Penalties—Yards	3-56

Rushing—Morris 20 for 105 yards, Csonka 20 for 73 yards, Kiick 10 for 52 yards, Leigh 1 for 8 yards, Nottingham 1 for 3 yards; Newhouse 10 for 54 yards, Dorsett 13 for 57 yards, Staubach 3 for 2 yards.

Passing—Griese 11 for 18 for 159 yards, one interception; Staubach 12 for 23 for 158 yards, one interception.

Receiving—Warfield 4 for 96 yards, Mandich 3 for 26 yards, Kiick 3 for 20 yards, Briscoe 1 for 17 yards; D. Pearson 4 for 5 yards, P. Pearson 3 for 47 yards, Richards 2 for 34 yards, Newhouse 1 for 6 yards, Dupree 1 for 15 yards, Dorsett 1 for 6 yards.

Semifinal: 1962 Green Bay vs. 1973 Oakland

In first round games, Green Bay won impressively, and Oakland pulled a minor upset in beating Pittsburgh. This game features two high-accuracy passers in Bart Starr and Ken Stabler. But Green Bay, with Jim Taylor's running, is given a slight edge.

Starr came out passing, hitting Ron Kramer over the middle for an 11-yard pass and a quick 7-0 lead. Early in the second quarter, Stabler hit three short passes and set up a five yard run by Clarence Davis, which tied it 7-7. Green Bay got a 21-yard field goal from Jim Kramer on their next possession, and held a 10-7 halftime lead.

No touchdowns were scored in the second half. Like two old stags, these teams locked horns in a defensive standoff. Oakland got an early George Blanda field goal to tie it, 10-10. The Packers went ahead 13-10 on a Jim Kramer 24-yard field goal. The big surprise was that there was no more scoring. Through the fourth quarter, Oakland moved the ball, but could not get close. Blanda missed two long field goal tries, and Green Bay squeaked through by the slimmest of margins.

```
1973 Oakland     0   7   3   0—10
1962 Green Bay   7   3   3   0—13
```

1st Q	GB	R. Kramer, 11 yd TD pass from Starr, PAT—J. Kramer (kick)
2nd Q	Oak	Davis, 5 yd TD rush, PAT—Blanda (kick)
	GB	J. Kramer, 21 yd field goal
3rd Q	Oak	Blanda, 17 yd field goal
	GB	J. Kramer, 24 yd field goal

Oakland		Green Bay
15	1st Downs	18
27-105	Rushing	46-159
15-127	Passing	10-106
89	Returns	84
15-23-1	Passes	22-10-0
4-52.5	Punts	5-31.2
1-0	Fumbles, Lost	2-0
3-36	Penalties—Yards	4-43

Rushing—Hubbard 11 for 53 yards, C. Smith 9 for 36 yards, C. Davis 4 for 14 yards, Banaszak 3 for 2 yards; Taylor 31 for 97 yards, Hornung 6 for 27 yards, Moore 8 for 33 yards, Starr 1 for 2 yards.

Passing—Stabler 15 for 23 for 127 yards, one interception; Starr 10 for 22 for 106 yards.

Receiving—C. Smith 4 for 34 yards, Siani 4 for 49 yards, Biletnikoff 4 for 31 yards, Hubbard 2 for 11 yards, Moore 1 for 2 yards; Dowler 4 for 47 yards, Taylor 2 for 13 yards, R. Kramer 3 for 32 yards, McGee 1 for 14 yards.

Final: 1962 Green Bay Packers vs. 1973 Miami Dolphins

The Lineups:

Green Bay 1962   *Miami 1973*

	Offense	
Max McGee	SE	Paul Warfield
Norm Masters	LT	Wayne Moore
Fuzzy Thurston	LG	Bob Keuchenberg
Jim Ringo	C	Jim Langer
Jerry Kramer	RG	Larry Little
Forest Gregg	RT	Norm Evans
Ron Kramer	TE	Jim Mandich
Bart Starr	Q	Bob Griese
Jim Taylor	FB	Larry Csonka
Tom Moore	HB	Mercury Morris
Boyd Dowler	FL	Marlin Briscoe

	Defense	
Willie Davis	LE	Vern Den Herder
Dave Hanner	LT	Manny Fernandez
Henry Jordan	RT	Larry Woods
Bill Quinlan	RE	Bill Stanfill
Dan Currie	LLB	Mike Kolen
Ray Nitschke	MLB	Nick Buoniconti
Bill Forester	RLB	Doug Swift
Herb Adderly	LCB	Tim Foley

Jesse Whittenton	RCB	Curtis Johnson
Hank Greminger	TS	Dick Anderson
Willie Wood	FS	Jake Scott

In the All-Time Pro Football Finals, it's Lombardi *vs*. Shula, Starr *vs*. Griese, and Taylor *vs*. Csonka. The best of the sixties versus the best of the seventies should be a classic struggle. Green Bay got to the finals by slaughtering Baltimore and squeaking past Oakland. Miami beat Minnesota in a tight defensive struggle, and then won easily against offensive-minded Dallas. The finals looks to be a titanic contest between two evenly-matched teams from different eras.

The All-Time Finals saw Green Bay win the coin toss and elect to receive. They took the ball and marched 98 yards on the ground. Jim Taylor ran in from the seven, and it was 7-0. Late in the quarter, Miami put together a march, with Csonka and Morris doing the damage. Csonka went over from the three, and it was tied.

In the second quarter, Taylor broke off tackle for a 35 yard score, and it was 14-7. Just before the half ended, the Dolphins marched again. Jim Kiick went over from the two, and it was 14-14 at halftime.

After receiving a punt in the third quarter, Starr put together some passes for a Green Bay score. Ron Kramer got the score on a 17-yard pass. Miami stalled, but Yepremian hit a 42-yard field goal that cut the Packer lead to 21-17. Jim Kramer got a field goal for Green Bay and it was 24-17 after three quarters.

Miami marched again in the fourth quarter and Csonka scored from the one. It was 24-24 with six minutes left. Green Bay then took five minutes to go 81 yards for a score, with Taylor going in from the three. Miami ran out of time, and the Green Bay Packers won the all-time title 31-24.

1962 Green Bay	7	7	10	7—31
1973 Miami	7	7	3	7—24

1st Q	GB	Taylor, 7 yd TD rush, PAT—J. Kramer (kick)
	Miami	Csonka, 3 yd TD rush, PAT—Yepremian (kick)
2nd Q	GB	Taylor, 35 yd TD rush, PAT—J. Kramer (kick)
	Miami	Kiick, 2 yd TD rush, PAT—Yepremian (kick)
3rd Q	GB	R. Kramer, 17 yd TD pass from Starr, PAT—J. Kramer (kick)
	Miami	Yepremian, 42 yd field goal
	GB	J. Kramer, 23 yd field goal
4th Q	Miami	Csonka, 1 yd TD rush, PAT—Yepremian (kick)
	GB	Taylor, 3 yd TD rush, PAT—J. Kramer (kick)

Green Bay		Miami
18	1st Downs	17
39-265	Rushing	38-236
73	Passing	35
135	Returns	197
8-12-0	Passes	5-9-0
2-38.0	Punts	4-41.2
3-1	Fumbles, Lost	2-0
4-40	Penalties—Yards	4-34

GB rushing—Taylor 26 for 157 yards, Moore 8 for 73 yards, Hornung 3 for 22 yards, Gros 2 for 13 yards.

Miami rushing—Csonka 20 for 151, Morris 9 for 53 yards, Kiick 5 for 19 yards, Nottingham 4 for 13 yards.

GB passing—Starr, 8 of 12 for 73 yards.

Miami passing—Griese, 5 of 9 for 35 yards.

GB pass receiving—McGee, 3 for 23 yards; Dowler 3 for 29 yards, R. Kramer 2 for 21 yards.

Miami pass receiving—Warfield, 1 for 15 yards, Kiick 2 for 7 yards, Briscoe 1 for 6 yards, Mandich 1 for 7 yards.

The all-time best professional football team is the best

team from the Lombardi-Packer years. In competition with the best teams of later years, Green Bay remained virtually unstoppable. Their unique blend of running, passing, defense, and all-around team depth proved they could compete with anyone.

We congratulate the 1962 Green Bay Packers and their late great coach Vince Lombardi. Vince once said, "Winning isn't everything; it's the only thing." Now, after winning in the all-time competition, Vince looks more and more like the best example of his winning philosophy. Since pro football is so complex and requires such an unusual mix of individual and group talents, this win represents one of the most memorable of the all-time matchups. The team and the coach will stand always among the greatest of the entire sports world.

The All-Time Stanley Cup Playoff (Hockey)

The Field

The National Hockey League boasts a history second only to baseball in professional team sports. It also awards to its best yearly team one of sports' most famous trophies—the Stanley Cup. The cup, donated by Lord Stanley of Canada in 1893 to reward professional supremacy in hockey, has been awarded to the best team in the National Hockey League, since 1918.

In the years since 1918, there have been many stand-out teams in the NHL. Some were impressive for one year, while others won two or three Cups in a row. One team, Montreal, has won four or more straight Cups on two different occasions. This team won five straight from 1956 to 1960 and four straight from 1976 to 1979. In this competition, those Montreal Canadien teams, and several others, will be vying for the All-Time Stanley Cup Prize.

For this competition, one of the most elaborate playoffs was devised. Twenty-three teams played a three out of five series in the first round. For round two, the twelve teams played a best four out of seven series. This reduced the field to the final six teams, the six best of all-time. Here is a preview of those six teams who will contend for the All-Time Stanley Cup.

1920 Ottawa Senators. This highest scoring NHL team won 79 percent of their games, scoring five goals a game while allowing 2.7. Their potent offense was led by the line of Jack Darragh, Frank Nighbor and Cy Dennenny, and backed by Punch Broadbent. The defense of Eddie Gerrard, George Boucher and rough Sprague Cleghorn fronted for goalie Clint Benedict. Benedict, an innovator, was the first to use a mask and one of the first to smother the puck, a practice that was legalized in 1918.

1939 Boston Bruins. The offense was led by the "Kraut Line" of Bobby Bauer, Milt Schmidt, and Woody Dumart from Kitchener, Ontario and directed by playmaker Bill Cowley. A rough-and-tumble classic team, they have the strongest defense in these finals. The defensive team was led by the great scoring defenseman Eddie Shore, who accumulated 958 stitches. The goalie was Frank Brimsek, the original "Mr. Zero," so-called because of his many shutouts.

1944 Montreal Canadiens. The offense was led by the great "Punch Line" of Toe Blake, Elmer Lach and "Rocket" Richard. The defense was headed by the non-scoring Butch Bouchard and the strong goal-tending of Bill Durnan. They boast the best win percentage (.830) and may shape up as one of the strongest teams.

1956 Montreal Canadiens. Coming from the time of the classic six-team league, they boasted a Hall-of-Fame offense of Jean Beliveau, "Boom-Boom" Geoffrion, "Rocket" Richard, Dickie Moore and Bert Olmstead. Their defensive specialist was Doug Harvey. Jacques Plante, who popularized the use of his own masks, was the goalie.

1972 Boston Bruins. Their all-star, Bobby Orr, was the first defenseman to score 100 points and win the scoring title. Teamed with Phil Esposito, the single season record holder, they comprised the best one-two punch in hockey history. Johnny Bucyk, Fred Stanfield, and Derek Sanderson complemented the scoring, but Gerry Cheevers and Eddie Johnston were not the strongest goalies.

1977 Montreal Canadiens. The expansion, which began in 1968, had threatened to dilute Montreal's traditional strength. But surviving wins by Boston in 1970 and '72, and

Philadelphia in 1974 and '75, Montreal re-established their dynasty. They had a record sixty wins, the second best percentage (.825), the best goal margin (2.7), and an overwhelming playoff (12-2). The lines of Guy Lafleur, Steve Shutt, Peter Mahovolich, Jacques Lemaire, Yvan Cournoyer, and Yvon Lambert, showed as much depth as any team in history. The defense of Serge Savard, Guy LaPointe, Larry Robinson, Bill Nyrop, and Pierre Bouchard was one of the best ever, and certainly the best scoring defense ever. Ken Dryden and sub Michel Laroque were probably the best goal defense to arise since the defensive-minded years. This was presumably the best of the many great Montreal teams, and maybe the best team of all-time.

As the teams enter the next round of playoffs, you may like to try picking the winner. Will it be the high-scoring, old-time Ottawa Senators? Perhaps the 1939 Bruins or the 1956 Canadiens from the days of classic, low scorning hockey will prevail. Could it be the 1944 Montreal team, who boast the best win percentage? The modern 1972 Bruins show great individual scoring punch. Will it carry them through to the title? Or will the overall depth of the 1977 Canadiens be the deciding factor?

The six teams will play a round-robin series, with the two best teams qualifying for the all-time final. The final will be a best six out of eleven series.

They're about to drop the puck. Who is your pick for the all-time best?

The Playoffs

Day 1

    (1) 1977 Montreal 4, 1972 Boston 3 (1st O.T.)
    (2) 1944 Montreal 2, 1956 Montreal 1
    (3) 1939 Boston 1, 1920 Ottawa 0

In three close games, things went about as expected. Montreal of 1977 had to go into overtime before Larry Robinson scored for the win.

Day 2

    (4) 1939 Boston 3, 1977 Montreal (1st O.T.)
    (5) 1944 Montreal 6, 1972 Boston 1
    (6) 1956 Montreal 1, 1920 Ottawa 0

The Canadiens of 1944 remained undefeated, while the Bruins of 1939 pulled an upset. Ottawa remained without a goal.

Day 3

    (7) 1977 Montreal 5, 1956 Montreal 4
    (8) 1972 Boston 2, 1939 Boston 1
    (9) 1944 Montreal 5, 1920 Ottawa 4

The games remained close, with Montreal of 1944 still undefeated. Montreal of 1977 and Boston of 1939 were tied with two victories each.

Day 4

    (10) 1944 Montreal 4, 1939 Boston 3
    (11) 1956 Montreal 3, 1972 Boston 2
    (12) 1977 Montreal 3, 1920 Ottawa 2

1944 Montreal remained undefeated (4-0) and clinched a berth in the finals. 1977 Montreal held in second (3-1). 1939 Boston (2-2) and 1956 Montreal (2-2) still had an outside chance for the finals. Two of the final three games became crucial. 1977 Montreal could assure themselves a spot in the finals if they beat undefeated Montreal of 1944. But, if Montreal of 1977 lost, then they would fall into a tie with the winner of the other key game between 1939 Boston and 1956 Montreal.

Day 5

    (13) 1977 Montreal 6, 1944 Montreal 5 (1st O.T.)
    (14) 1939 Boston 3, 1956 Montreal 0
    (15) 1920 Ottawa 5, 1972 Boston 0

1977 Montreal did what they had to do, beating the previously undefeated 1944 Canadiens, and skated into the All-Time Playoffs against them.

The win did not come easily and depended on overtime action. In period one, the 1977 team went up 2-0 on goals by Lafleur and Lemaire. Hefferman scored twice for the 1944 team to make it 2-2. Shutt put the 1977 team up 3-2 to close out a hectic first period. Robinson scored the only goal in period two, making it 4-2.

In period three, Lach and Blake scored to make it 4-4. Lemaire put the 1977 team ahead 5-4, but Lach scored on a power play, sending the game into overtime. The 1944 team got no shots in the overtime, as Shutt put in the winning goal. The 1977 team could now look forward to a best of eleven series against this same team, their strong forerunners from the same franchise.

Round Robin Standing

	W	L
77 Montreal	4	1
44 Montreal	4	1
39 Boston	3	2
56 Montreal	2	3
20 Ottawa	1	4
72 Boston	1	4

The stage is set for the All-Time Hockey Playoff series. The best of eleven game series looks to be a real slash, bang, all-out offensive war. The 1944 Canadiens have two of the top scorers, Toe Blake and Elmer Lach. On the other hand, the 1977 team has more balanced scoring, with defenseman Larry Robinson supplementing the front line. Because both goalies have given up lots of goals, the series promises a lot of scoring.

Final: 1977 Montreal vs. 1944 Montreal

First Game: 1977 (4), 1944 (2)

In the first game of the All-Time Playoff, 1977 Montreal fell behind in period one, but went ahead 2-1 in the second. On Shutt's second goal in period three, the 1977 team went up 3-1 and held on to win 4-2.

1st Period	1. Hefferman (10) '44
2nd Period	2. Lemaire (11) '77, 3. Shutt (15) '77
3rd Period	4. Shutt (16) '77, 5. Getliffe (10) '44, 6. Cournoyer (2) '77

Second Game: 1977 (5), 1944 (4)

Montreal of 1977 went up 3-0 in period one, but were tied up 4-4 in period three by the 1944 team's second power play goal. Lafleur then scored off of Robinson and Savard for the win.

1st Period	1. Robinson (5) '77, 2. Cournoyer (3) '77, 3. Cournoyer (4) '77, 4. Hefferman (11) '44
2nd Period	5. Blake (12) '44, 6. Richard (14) '44, 7. Cournoyer (5) '77
3rd Period	8. Watson (7) '44, 9. Lafleur (11) '77

Third Game: 1977 (4), 1944 (3)

Montreal of 1944 had been outshot by seventeen more shots on goal in the first two games and came out to play a more controlled third game. The control was there but the team fell behind 1-3 in period two, and lost after drawing even in the last period.

1st Period	1. Lafleur (12) '77, 2. Blake (13) '44
2nd Period	3. Shutt (17) '77, 4. Shutt (18) '77
3rd Period	5. Watson (8) '44, 6. Hefferman (12) '44, 7. Lambert (1) '77

Fourth Game: 1977 (4), 1943 (3) (1st Overtime)

Trailing by 3-0 in games, the 1944 Canadians tried to maintain a controlled game, and succeeded to some extent. It was 3-3 after regulation, but the 1977 Montreal team won in overtime, taking a commanding four games to none lead.

1st Period	1. Shutt (19) '77, 2. Lafleur (13) '77, 3. Hefferman (13) '44
2nd Period	None
3rd Period	4. Majeau (6) '44, 5. Hefferman (14) '44, 6. Lemaire (12) '77
1st O.T.	7. Robinson (6) '77

Fifth Game: 1944 (7), 1977 (4)

Trailing 4-0 games, the '44 team played control to perfection, winning with 7 goals out of 26 shots.

1st Period	1. Getliffe (11) '44, 2. Houle (1) '77, 3. Richard (15) '44
2nd Period	4. Cournoyer (6) '77, Nyrop (1) '77, 6. McMahon (3) '44, 7. Majeau (7) '44
3rd Period	8. Lach (9) '44, 9. Richard (16) '44, 10. Majeau (8) '44, 11. Lapointe (4) '77

Sixth Game: 1977 (4), 1944 (3)

For the first time in the series, the 1944 team shot more than thirty times. But their 36 shots produced only 3 goals, and they fell behind five games to one. Shutt's twentieth playoff goal won it.

1st Period	1. Richard (17) '44, 2. Lambert (2) '77, 3. Jarvis (1) '77
2nd Period	4. Richard (18) '44, 5. Mahovlovich (1) '77, 6. Lach (10) '44
3rd Period	7. Shutt (20) '77

Seventh Game: 1944 (3), 1977 (1)

Just one game away from elimination, the 1944 Canadiens held the 1977 team to just one goal, winning on the strength of two Hefferman goals.

1st Period	No score
2nd Period	1. Lafleur (14) '77, 2. Hefferman (15) '44
3rd Period	3. Getliffe (12) '44, 4. Hefferman (16) '44

Eighth Game: 1944 (7), 1977 (4)

The '44 Canadiens scored five times in period three, running away with the game. They brought the series record to 3-5, and still hung on. Toe Blake made three goals.

1st Period	1. Lapointe (5) '77, 2. Hefferman (17) '44, 3. Houle (2) '77
2nd Period	4. Savard (1) '77, 5. Blake (14) '44
3rd Period	6. Blake (15) '44, 7. Lemaire (13) '77, 8. Watson (9) '44, 9. Watson (1) '44 10. Blake (16) '44, 11. Hefferman (18) '44

Ninth Game: 1977 (7), 1944 (2)

The 1977 Montreal Canadiens came out quickly, and wrapped up the All-Time Playoff six games to three. The outcome had been evident since the third or fourth game; 1977 Montreal established themselves as the all-time best. The team that had been master of the close game and the come-from-behind victory rode balanced scoring to a runaway win.

1st Period	1. Lemaire (14) '77, 2. Lafleur (15) '77, 3. Lafleur (16) '77, 4. Lapointe (6) '77
2nd Period	5. Cournoyer (7) '77, 6. Lemaire (15) '77
3rd Period	7. Lach (11) '44, 8. Tremblay (1) '77, 9. O'Connor (2) '44

Leaders After the Finals

	GP	G	A	TP
Lafleur, '77 Montreal	18	16	29	45
Blake, '44 Montreal	22	16	28	44
Lach, '44 Montreal	22	11	30	41
Shutt, '77 Montreal	18	20	14	34
Orr, '72 Boston	15	12	21	33

Lemaire, '77 Montreal	18	15	17	32
R. Richard, '44 Montreal	22	18	13	31
Robinson, '77 Montreal	18	6	24	30
Esposito, '72 Boston	15	12	15	27
Hefferman, '44 Montreal	22	18	7	25
Beliveau, '56 Montreal	15	11	14	25
Watson, '44 Montreal	22	8	16	24
O'Connor, '44 Montreal	22	2	21	23
Geoffrion, '60 Montreal	10	7	15	22
Getliffe, '44 Montreal	22	12	10	22
Lapointe, '77 Montreal	18	6	15	21
Nighbor, '20 Ottawa	14	12	8	20

Goalie Leaders After the Finals

	GP	GA	AVE	SHUT-OUTS
Brimsek, '39 Boston	13	8	0.62	7
Thompson, '19 Boston	8	12	1.50	2
Plante, '56 Montreal	15	25	1.66	4
Benedict, '20 Ottawa	14	32	2.29	1
Parent, '74 Philadelphia	10	24	2.40	1
Durnan, '44 Montreal	22	69	3.14	1
Dryden, '77 Montreal	18	57	3.16	1

The 1977 Montreal Canadiens stand as the All-Time Best Professional Hockey Team. We are indeed fortunate to have the All-Time Best playing before us now. This latest incarnation of the Montreal dynasty has continued its winning ways, playing at or near the level that made it the best.

It is unfortunate that Montreal does not get the television exposure of a few years back, for the team truly deserves it. We take off our hats to the "hat trick" skaters, the stars of the ice who stand as the best of the best.

The All-Time Soccer Playoff

The Field

Four teams were selected for the all-time soccer tournament from countries that participated in the World Cup games from 1930 to 1974. Entries were not limited to World Cup winners, as the best teams are sometimes upset and location has an overwhelming influence on who wins in soccer. The four best teams were judged on their overall performance and offensive and defensive play, in relation to the quality of their opposition and quantity of overall talent at the time. As a result of this elaborate evaluation process, such high-scoring teams as West Germany and Hungary of 1954 did not qualify because of their weaker defenses. The teams of 1930, 1934, and 1938 did not face the quantity of talent present since 1950 and also did not qualify any entrants.

Here is a preview of the four finalists in the All-Time Soccer Playoffs:

1958 Brazil

Brazil won the World Cup by beating the home country, Sweden, 5-2 in the finals. They finished the season undefeated and with one tie game against England. Brazil's World Cup victory introduced the 17-year-old Pele to the world. This was a sparkling offensive team, including Vava, Didi, and Zagalo as attackers and N. Santos on defense.

1966 England

Coached by Alf Ramsey, England took the Cup in a home country win by playing a defensive, error-free, no-nonsense game. If England had a star, it was the attacker Hurst. However, team play was their strength. Tied once by Uruguay, they beat West Germany 4-2 in overtime during the finals.

1974 West Germany

A slight favorite in 1974, West Germany won at home over a strong Dutch team that had captured the crowd's imagination. Muller, Beckenbauer, and Breitner led a sound defensive team that seemed to win, but not dazzle, the opposition. Losing early to East Germany, West Germany then defied all odds by beating Holland 2-1 in the finals.

1974 Holland

If there was any team that could compare with the exciting, offensive Brazilian style of play, it was the Dutch. Cruyff, the heir-apparent to Pele, and Neeskens led a strong passing attack. Tied by Sweden, the Dutch team was around the goal all day, but lost the breaks and the game to West Germany 1-2 in the finals. However, many thought they were the better team and Cruyff the top player in the world.

Usual Lineups: (goalies; fullbacks, halfbacks; forwards)

Brazil 1958
Gilmar; de Sordi, N. Santos; Zito; Bellini, Orlando; Garrincha, Didi, Vava, Pele, Zagalo.

England 1966
Banks; Cohen, J. Charlton; Moore, Wilson, Stiles; B. Charlton, Ball, Hurst, Hunt, Peters.

West Germany 1974
Maier; Vogts, Breitner; Beckenbauer, Schwarzenback, Honess; Grabowski, Bonhof, Muller, Overath, Holzenbien.

Holland 1974
Jongbloed; Suurbier, Krol; Jansen, Rijsbergen, Haan; Rep, Neeskens, Cruyff, Van Hanegem, Resenbrink.

Play is set for round-robin competition with each team to meet the other contestants one time. Two points will be given for a win, one point for a tie. If there is a tie after round-robin play, a playoff will be held.

The Tournament

Game One: Brazil 4, Holland 1

Halftime—Brazil 1, Holland 0. Brazil was around the goal the first half with mid-range shots by Didi and Vava. Vava also worked in close but missed his shot, and Garrincha failed on a rebound. One minute before the half, Pele sailed a long shot past Jongbloed into the net for a 1-0 halftime lead. Pele opened the second half with a shot that Jongbloed saved. Hiss pass out was stolen by Orlando, who made it 2-0 to virtually seal the victory seven minutes into the half. Undaunted, the Dutch came back quickly with Neeskens shooting on goal. Gilmar saved, but fouled and Cruyff put in a penalty kick to make it 2-1. Brazil came right back with Pele shooting and Zagalo putting in a rebound. After the kick, Pele stole the ball and shot long to make it 4-1. In the final twenty-two minutes, Neeskeens shot twice and Cruyff once, but the Brazilians held on easily for the win.

Game Two: England 1, West Germany 0

Halftime—no score. Geoff Hurst got off a shot for England thirteen minutes into the half and Bobby Moore missed a rebound shot before Germany shut them down. For Germany, Schwarzenbeck, Overath, and Grabowski all missed and Holzenbien failed on a corner kick. In the second half, Muller, Holzenbien, and Breitner all failed for Germany. Cohen missed an early shot and Moore a rebound for England's only effort until late in the game. Cohen got loose for a saved shot. Ball followed with a corner kick which John Charlton headed past goalie Maier, forty-two minutes into the half, for the win.

Game Three: Brazil 2, West Germany 0

Halftime—Brazil 1, West Germany 0. It was Vava's game. He had two missed shots off his own effort and a rebound off de Sordi's shot, giving Brazil a 1-0 lead at the half. Six minutes into the second half, Vava scored on another rebound of a de Sordi shot for the victory. From there on Brazil never shot. Germany got off five shots, three by Muller, as well as a corner kick by Bonhof. However, Brazil held on, showing they also could play defense.

Game Four: England 1, Holland 1

Halftime—England 1, Holland 1. Cohen shot early and missed, then scored in close, to give England a 1-0 lead. Neeskens took the kick-off down for a good mid-range shot to tie it at 1-1. Rijsbergen had two misses for Holland and Stiles missed one for England to close out the half. The second half saw only a shot by Hurst on England's kickoff and one by Holland's Jansen with a minute to go. In extra time, Holland got off only one shot, while Stiles shot twice and Hurst once for England. No one scored and it was a draw. By failing to win, England fell into second place in the round-robin play behind Brazil.

Game Five: West Germany 3, Holland 2

Halftime—West Germany 2, Holland 2. Each team scored the first two times it had the ball. Neeskens took the kick-off down and made a mid-range shot past Maier. Germany came back with Schwarzenbeck scoring on a rebound after a Muller shot. Neeskens repeated his first scoring maneuver. Muller again took a shot, and, this time, Bonhop rebounded it in to make it 2-2 eighteen minutes into the half. Holland's Jansen had the only other shot of the half—a miss. In the second half, Muller and Schwarzenbeck missed and Overath scored for Germany's 3-2 win. Holland played too conservatively and did not even get off a shot.

Game Six: Brazil 0, England 0

Overtime Game. Going into the final game of round-robin play, it was clear that no playoff would be necessary. This would be the final game since Brazil had a one point lead (owing to their two wins) against England's one win and one draw. The winner would be the all-time best. However, if there was a draw, Brazil would be the winner. With England needing a win and Brazil only a tie, would Brazil change their usually reckless offensive style? The statistics show that a total of fourteen shots were taken—certainly not a dull defensive battle. But none scored.

Pele opened with a missed shot and Zagalo missed a rebound for Brazil. Bellini also missed and Hunt got in a late first half shot from Hurst. In the second half, Zagalo, Bellini, and Pele missed early for Brazil and Cohen missed twice for England late in the game. Early in overtime, England's best chance saw Hurst shoot at mid-range, Hunt try a rebound, and Hurst follow his rebound. All missed and England went twenty-two minutes without another shot. With twelve minutes to go, Pele missed, and with one minute left, Orlando missed from long range. Brazil did not play conservatively and got off eight shots. Although the South Americans could not score in this one, the brilliance of Pele and overall team play established them as the best. Pele's play in two games and Vava's in the other one gave Brazil a one-two punch that no other team could challenge.

Final Rankings

	W	D	L	Pts	(GF)	(GA)
1. Brazil	2	1	0	5	6	1
2. England	1	2	0	4	2	1
3. West Germany	1	0	2	2	3	5
4. Holland	0	1	2	1	4	8

GF: Goals For
GA: Goals Against

The All-Time Heavyweight
Boxing Tournament

The Field

The holder of the heavyweight title has always occupied a unique position in the world of sports. Since John L. Sullivan announced, ''I can lick any man in the house,'' it has generally been assumed that, braggart or not, the heavyweight champ is better than the rest of us.

Not only is the heavyweight champ superior to the rest of us, but he has the ability to evoke emotional response. Men such as John Sullivan, Jack Johnson, Jack Dempsey, Max Baer, Joe Louis, Rocky Marciano, and Muhammad Ali have made people talk about them, write about them, praise and degrade them.

Now, in this all-time tournament, we have the opportunity to see all of the best heavyweight champs compete against each other, as they would have competed when they were at their peaks. Here are the results of the preliminary rounds in the all-time tournament:

Preliminary Round—Each winner advances to meet one of the eight seeded boxers.

Winner	Result	Loser	Rounds	Knockdowns
Max Baer	W15	Ezzard Charles	9-5	
George Foreman	TKO1	Jimmy Ellis	—	
Jim Corbett	W15	Jack Sharkey	10-5	
Bob Fitzsimmons	KO3	Jim Braddock	1-1	
Jess Willard	TKO6	Floyd Patterson	3-1	

Winner	Result	Loser	Rounds	Knockdowns
Max Schmeling	KO13	Tommy Burns	6-4	Burns down in 12
Sonny Liston	KO1	Ingemar Johansson	—	
Jersey Joe Walcott	TKO11	Primo Carnera	8-2	Carnera down in 3, 5, (3 times), 11

Second Round

Winner	Result	Loser	Rounds	Knockdowns
Muhammad Ali	KO15	Max Baer	8-5	
Jack Dempsey	KO1	George Foreman	—	Dempsey down in 1
Gene Tunney	TKO13	Jim Corbett	9-3	Corbett down in 7
Jack Johnson	TKO9	Bob Fitzsimmons	8-0	Fitzsimmons down in 1 & 9
Rocky Marciano	TKO7	Sonny Liston	6-0	
Joe Louis	KO4	Jess Willard	3-0	
Joe Frazier	TKO6	Max Schmeling	5-0	Schmeling down in 6
Jim Jeffries	W15	Joe Walcott	11-4	

The eight seeded heavyweights have survived the preliminary rounds and are now ready to enter the last rounds of competition for the all-time title. Here is a preview of the eight greatest heavyweights who will slug it out for the all-time title.

Jim Jeffries (6'2½", 220; 20-2-2, 16 KO's) This barrel-chested, ex-boilermaker fought out of a crouch and was the roughest slugger of his day. He held the title from 1899 to 1904 and had duel wins over Corbett, Fitzsimmons, and Tom Sharkey. Six years after his retirement, he lost to Jack Johnson.

Jack Johnson (6'¼", 222; 78-7-28, 44 KO's) The first black champion was a defensive boxer who won the title late in his career, after being refused earlier title shots. He was champ from 1908 to 1915. He beat the smaller boxers Hart, Burns, and Fitzsimmons and the aged Jeffries, before losing the title to Willard at age 37.

Jack Dempsey (6'1", 190; 60-7-14, 49 KO's) The first boxer to draw a million dollar gate, he had great public appeal based on many first round KO's of lesser opposition. He held the title from 1919 to 1926, losing to Tunney in a 10 round decision.

Gene Tunney (6'½", 190; 56-1-19, 41 KO's) Primarily a light heavyweight, he lost only once to the great middleweight Harry Greb. Tunney had only three years and seven bouts as a heavyweight, with his two clever decisions over Dempsey being his main claim to fame.

Joe Louis (6'1½", 200; 68-3-0, 54 KO's) He held the title for the longest consecutive time, 1937 to 1948, but fought only four times between 1943 and 1949. A devastating puncher with a straightforward, methodical style, he was troubled by boxers Billy Conn, Bob Pastor, and Tommy Farr and the unorthodox Arturo Godoy.

Rocky Marciano (5'11", 184; 49-0-0, 43 KO's) The only undefeated heavyweight champ, he held the title from 1952 to 1955. He beat an over-the-hill Louis, and had two wins over both Walcott and Charles. He was a swarming, untutored brawler.

Muhammad Ali (6'3", 215; 56-4-0, 37 KO's) A master boxer and the fastest heavyweight champ, he held the title three times; 1964-70, '74-78, '78-79. With two wins over Liston, Patterson and Frazier, and his upset of Foreman, he has the best record vs. other champs. He was troubled by Frazier and Ken Norton, both of whom kept the pressure on him continually.

Joe Frazier (5'11½", 205; 32-4-0, 27 KO's) A swarming body puncher, slightly larger than Marciano, he held the title from 1970 to 1973. He gave Ali trouble, winning one out of three, but Foreman's power twice destroyed him.

The Pairings for the Quarterfinals

Marciano vs. Ali

Tunney vs. Frazier

Jeffries vs. Johnson

Dempsey vs. Louis

The final eight include three kinds of boxers—the points scoring boxers, Tunney and Ali, the defensive Johnson, and the remaining five who are all sluggers. The heavyweight division is known for its power hitters. Will one of the big hitters take the title or will one of the other three nullify their power?

Who is your pick to win the all-time title? Johnson, Dempsey, Louis, Marciano, and Ali all have received critical and popular support as the all-time best. Dempsey and Louis meet in the quarter finals. The winner of that bout will take a big step toward the all-time title. Will it be a favorite or will an underdog pull an upset? Will it be a boxer or a slugger? Make your pick. Here come the finals:

The Tournament

Quarterfinals: Ali TKO11 Marciano

This bout featured two boxers who retired undefeated. Ali took charge of the bout, flooring Rocky in the second, fifth, and eleventh rounds. He led, eight rounds to two, when the referee stopped it in the eleventh.

Quarterfinals: Tunney W15 Frazier

In this battle of the boxer versus the swarmer, Frazier dropped Tunney in the sixth and ninth rounds. But Tunney's boxing held off Frazier as Gene won a decision: nine rounds to four, with two even.

Quarterfinals: Dempsey W15 Louis

In this all-time power matchup, Dempsey started early, dropping Louis in the first round. Joe survived and came back to score a knockdown in round six. From then on, it became a boxing match, and Dempsey won nine rounds to six.

Quarterfinals: Johnson W15 Jeffries

In this replay of an historical bout, Jeffries would now be boxing at his peak. Johnson took control, and outpointed Jeffries ten rounds to five. Unable to stop Jeffries as quickly as he did when Jeffries was past his peak, Johnson nevertheless won easily.

Semi-finals: Muhammad Ali vs. Gene Tunney

This is a classic matchup between two premier boxers with similar styles. The differences are that Ali had superior size and a much longer heavyweight career. Tunney had been a light-heavy for all but seven bouts of his career.

Round 1—Ali led with a stinging right cross. Tunney danced at long range and scored with two lefts. Tunney scored with a left and a hard right. Tunney jabbed lightly and missed with a wild hook.

Round 2—Tunney landed a stiff right and pawed with his left in a slow round.

Round 3—Tunney pawed and threw a jab. Ali jabbed, stopped, and stung Tunney with a hard right, and jabbed hard as Tunney danced away.

Round 4—Tunney scored two light lefts and then landed a stiff left as Ali waited. Tunney appeared to have a slight lead.

Round 5—Tunney threw two lefts. Ali landed a left and a strong right uppercut to stop Tunney in his tracks.

Round 6—Tunney threw a left and then jabbed lightly. Ali stepped up the pace, jabbing lightly and stinging with a right cross. Ali jabbed hard, then scored with another hard right.

Round 7—Ali led off with another stinging right, which Tunney seemed unable to stop. Both danced. Tunney got in two jabs and a right, but Ali punished Tunney with two hard rights. Ali now seemed to dominate Tunney.

Round 8—Ali became aggressive. They traded rights. Ali danced and jabbed as Tunney got in a right. Tunney jabbed lightly and scored with a right. Ali matched him with a stinging jab and another hard right. It was a close round.

Round 9—Tunney tried to hold Ali's arms, then landed a jab when Ali went on his bicycle. Ali coasted.

Round 10—Tunney jabbed lightly, then stiffly. Both danced, then Ali moved Tunney against the ropes and landed a hard right.

Round 11—Sensing Ali was leading slightly, Tunney tried to step up the pace. They traded left-rights in ring center, then Ali danced away. Tunney caught Ali with a left hook and dropped him for a three count. Ali took the standing eight count and seemed to be bleeding at the nose. Ali opened up with a stinging right, and a jab bloodied Tunney's nose. Ali jabbed hard and danced away. Tunney stung Ali with a hard right and Ali clinched at the bell.

Round 12—With the bout about even, Tunney opened up aggressively, landing with two stiff rights. Ali went up on his toes and danced to his left, throwing long stinging lefts —one-two-three-four. Tunney couldn't reach him. More lefts—one-two-three. Suddenly, Ali set himself and stung Tunney with a vicious right. Tunney was hurt and his nose bled again.

Round 13—Both boxers danced at long range. Ali stung with a left and Tunney pawed lightly. Ali danced, while Tunney scored with two jabs and then pawed lightly.

Round 14—With the bout still up for grabs, Ali went on the attack. He landed a six blow left-right combination and Tunney reeled against the ropes. Ali stung him with another hard right and a left. Tunney was done in, but holding on.

Round 15—Ali led with a strong left and pushed Tunney to the ropes. He stung Tunney with a right to the jaw and leaned into him on the ropes. Sensing victory, Ali held on, with Tunney unable to score at all.

Decision: Rounds 8-6-1, Ali W15. Ali had a slight edge in points and power, though he did hit the canvas once.

Semifinals: Jack Dempsey vs. Jack Johnson

One of the greatest sluggers of all time, Jack Dempsey will battle perhaps the greatest defensive boxer ever, Jack Johnson.

Round 1—Dempsey charged and scored with a hard right to the head. They traded jabs, and Johnson stung Dempsey with a right to the forehead. Dempsey showed a left eye cut. Dempsey scored a left-right-left, then Johnson began to pick off Dempsey's blows. They traded jabs and Johnson blocked Dempsey again. Johnson stung Dempsey with a right uppercut and was blocking Dempsey's blows at the bell.

Round 2—Dempsey scored two rights and then a jab as Johnson waited.

Round 3—Dempsey came out aggressively, landed a left jab, and then got in a hard right that dropped Johnson for the full count.

Decision: Dempsey KO3, 1:53.

Finals: Muhammad Ali vs. Jack Dempsey

The all-time finals will be a classic boxer-slugger struggle. In beating Tunney, Ali showed he was the best boxer and exhibited some power. Dempsey was devastating in taking out the defensive master Jack Johnson. It's speed and size versus power for the all-time final.

Round 1—Dempsey moved in close and missed a wild right. Ali danced at long range and popped Dempsey's face with jabs—one-two-three at a time. Ali stung Dempsey with a right cross. Dempsey charged in. Ali caught him with a right uppercut and dropped him for an eight count. The bell sounded before Ali could follow up.

Round 2—Ali danced at long range. Dempsey scored with a leaping right and Ali's nose trickled blood. Ali stung Dempsey with a vicious left-right-left which stopped Dempsey in his tracks. Dancing at long range, Ali did not follow up, but kept Dempsey away.

Round 3—Ali circled left at long range, jabbing lightly. Dempsey got in a jab. Ali danced, missed a wild right, and jabbed some more. Ali got in a right on the right eye and Dempsey began to puff up.

Round 4—Dempsey charged out, but Ali met him with a hard right and Dempsey's nose bled. Dempsey jabbed and missed a wild right. Ali danced and stung Dempsey with another stiff right and Dempsey looked puffy under both eyes.

Round 5—Ali continued to dance and sting Dempsey with lefts three at a time. Dempsey got in a jab. Ali continued to dance and flick out jabs. Ali missed with two wild rights at the bell. It was all Ali through five rounds.

Round 6—Ali danced at long range as Dempsey missed a wild right. Dempsey scored with a jab. Ali stung Dempsey with a right, and Dempsey's nose bled again. Ali hit Dempsey with a left-right combination and thoroughly controlled him.

Round 7—Dempsey charged out and got in a stiff right. Ali stood flat-footed and blasted Dempsey with a hard left-right-left. Dempsey jabbed twice to the stalking Ali, but Ali drove Dempsey to the ropes with a stunning left-right-left at the bell.

Round 8—Ali again danced and Dempsey could not touch him. Ali stung Dempsey with a right and his nose bled again. Ali danced and then stopped to throw a tremendous left-right-left which staggered Dempsey. Surprisingly, Ali went back to dancing, but stopped to deliver another left-right-left, which draped Dempsey over the ropes at the bell.

Round 9—As round nine began, Ali had apparently won every round and decided to let up. Dempsey scored with a right and a left and missed a wild right as Ali moved away.

Dempsey scored a left-right, and another left, and Ali's nose bled.

Round 10—Ali went back to work stunning Dempsey with a three blow combination. Then Ali began to dance, and Dempsey got in a strong right. Both missed wild rights. Ali continued dancing. Dempsey leaped in with a jab and a left-right and Ali's nose bled again.

Round 11—With Ali flat-footed, Dempsey jabbed, and then punished him with three blows to the body. Ali scored a hard right, but Dempsey jabbed twice and worked three more to the body.

Round 12—Dempsey rushed out, but Ali met him with a stiff jab. A left-right-left drove Dempsey to the ropes. Ali jabbed the defenseless Dempsey and stung him with a right on the ropes, but then backed away.

Round 13—As the round began, Dempsey apparently needed a knockout to win. He charged, working hard to Ali's body while Ali covered up. Dempsey jabbed Ali and then caught him with a right, which dropped Ali as he retreated. Ali took an eight count as the bell sounded.

Round 14—Ali missed a knockout attempt with a wild right. Ali danced away. Dempsey bulled him to the ropes, landing heavy to the body as Ali held his arms.

Round 15—Dempsey charged out to try for a KO, but was not quick enough to be effective. Ali let himself be blasted with lefts and rights to the body. The referee broke them and Ali stayed on the ropes. Dempsey swung lefts and rights to the head, backed off, jabbed and then landed a left-right-left to the head at the bell.

Decision: 9 rounds to 6, Ali W15.

Ali took the play away from Dempsey in the first eight rounds and then boxed defensively to win by decision. Dempsey was able to punish the tiring Ali to the body, but could not hit him often enough in the head to get the knockout he needed. Again Ali survived a knockdown to get the win.

"I am the greatest," he used to cry, for the purposes of advertising his art. Later he told us he didn't mean it. But by then it was too late; people had begun to believe he really was the greatest.

Now we have the all-time tournament based on thousands of preliminary results as well as the final matchups. Who emerges as the best?—the one who bragged that he was.

Muhammad Ali won the all-time title primarily by outpointing his opponents. In the heavyweight division where knockouts are the rule, Ali broke the mold in winning. This was not the slower, more powerful Ali who had beaten Frazier and Foreman in his later career. The winner was that flicking, jabbing, dancing young Ali of 1963 to 1967 who may not have been able to KO his opponents, but who could outrun and outpoint anyone. That younger Ali, "the Louisville Lip," the brash young predictor, beat them all. All hail Ali—you really are the greatest.

The All-Time Bowling Tournament

The Field

Mention bowling and the average man on the street turns his head. Other sports he identifies with, but this one he plays. It is probably the number one participation sport.

The All-Time Bowling Tournament brings together the top eleven high rollers of all time. They are the ones with the best reputations in the sport. Obviously at their peak, they are in a class by themselves. However, on a bad night, a mere mortal might possibly upset them. Here is a preview of the illustrious field. You'll have to write your own scenario if you plan to take on the winner.

Andrew Varipapa (Andy). The oldest performer in the field built his reputation as an instructor, exhibition bowler, and trick-shot artist. Bowler of the Year in 1948, he won the All-Star title in '47 and '48 at the age 55 and 56. Boasting one 300 game, he is rated on the 1932-33 season when his average was 217.

Walter G. Ward. An early bowling star, he had twelve 300 games, four 800 series, and a best series of 836. Rated on the 1933-34 season, he has the third best average in the tournament at 230.

Steve Joseph Nagy. The first famous 1950's bowler, he won Bowler of the Year in 1952 and '55. He had six 300's, four 299's, and a best series of 831. He is rated on the 1952-53 season with a 217 average.

Alfred Joseph Faragalli (Lindy). One of the highest rollers, he boasts fourteen 300's, five 800's, and a best series of 828. He is rated on the 1953-54 season with a 229 average, which is fourth best in the field.

William Terrell Lillard (Bill). Bowler of the Year in 1956, he had four 300's and a best series of 782. He is rated on the 1956-57 season with a 223 average.

Raymond Albert Bluth (Bleep). He has twelve 300 games, five 800's series, and a best series of 834, second best in the field. He is rated on the 1956-57 season with a 226 average.

Donald James Carter. The accomplishments of Carter are many. He won Bowler of the Year six times between 1953 and '62. He took the World Invitational five times in six years between 1957 and '62. He was the first to win bowling's "Grand Slam" in 1961. In 1970 he was voted the greatest bowler in history by *Bowling Magazine.* He has thirteen 300's and five 800 series, with a high of 824. He is rated on the 1957-58 season when he averaged 232, the tops in the field.

Robert H. Strampe (Bob). A model of consistency, he boasts the best five-year average (216) and ten-year average (212) between 1961 and '71. He had six 300's and series of 833 and 804. He is rated on the 1958-59 season when he averaged 214.

Richard Anthony Weber (Dick). Consistently the leading tournament money winner, with $397,000 official earnings, Weber won over $500,000 total. Bowler of the Year in 1961, '63, and '65, he won the most PBA titles—24 in fourteen years. He was known for his ability to adjust his delivery at the foul line. He rolled seventeen 300's and four 800 series, with 815 his best. Though he was Mr. Bowling in the 1960's, he is rated in the 1975 season with a 213 average.

Eddie Lubanski. Boasting the highest lifetime average, a 204 over twenty-five years, he is a strong contender for the all-time title. Using the old style two-finger ball, he rolled eleven 300 games and three 800's, with a best of 815. He is rated on the 1959-60 season with a 231 average, the second best in the field.

Earl Anthony. A left-hander, he boasts career earnings of

$600,000. He has twelve 300 games, three 800 series, and his 838 is the best in this star-studded field. The most recent super bowler, he is rated on the 1975 season when he averaged 219.

Countless other famous bowlers are left out who have made major contributions to the game. These include Ned Day, Dolph Carlson, Hank Marino, Louis Campi, Buddy Bomar, Billy Hardwick, Don Johnson, Buzz Fazio, Bob Pinkalla, Elvin Mesger, John Gengler, Walter Mercurio, Alfie Conn and famous women Floretta McCutcheon and Marion Ladewig. The list could go on forever.

Certainly these near greats, and numerous other bowlers, could have beaten the top eleven occasionally. However, judging by average score, length of career, and overall reputation in the sport, these top eleven were chosen as those most worthy to contend for the all-time title.

Who will be the all-time best bowler? The top four averages belong to Carter, Lubanski, Ward, and Farragalli. Will they play consistently in the pressure cooker of the all-time tournament? Weber has the most 300 games and PBA titles. He was also a big money winner but without a great average. How will he do? Earl Anthony has the best three game score and is the best recent money player, but, again, his average is topped by several bowlers. Will Lubanski's highest lifetime average help carry him to the all-time championship? Bob Strampe has the five-year and ten-year average records but his rated average for this tournament is one of the lowest.

The tournament seems wide open. It would appear to be a contest between two groups—the high average group versus the big money winners, Carter, Weber, and Anthony. Carter is the only member of both groups, but that is no guarantee of victory.

As they set up the pins, who do you pick as bowling's all-time champ?

The Finals

Don Carter justified his selection as the greatest bowler in history by winning the all-time tournament. An opening game of 217 placed him 39 pins back, and tied for fifth. He then put together two games of 236 for a 689 total and the win. Five other bowlers had better individual games, but Carter fashioned the best three game total.

Game one was taken by Lindy Faragalli, who rolled 256. He had strikes in the first five frames, frame nine, and the first two shots in frame ten. He was followed by Walter Ward with a 245 and Bill Lillard with a 237.

Earl Anthony's 238 won the second game. He had eight strikes, including frames three through six. Ray Bluth at 237 and Carter at 236 were close behind. After two games the leaders were:

1. Farragalli   459
2. Lillard   454
3. Carter   453
4. Ward   452

The great first games of Farragalli, Ward, and Lillard kept them on top. Carter was mounting a charge, but it was still wide open among the four leaders.

In game three, Carter wasted little time in taking over the lead. With a strike in frame two, compared with spares for Lillard and Farragalli, Carter went into the lead and never lost it. With six strikes, he rolled 236 and beat everyone in the final game.

Anthony was second at 217 and sixth overall. Lubanski had his second 216, placing third for the game and third overall. Farragalli had a 207 and clung to second in the overall standings.

Final Standings All-Time Bowling Tournament

1.	Don Carter	689	(217, 236, 236)
2.	Lindy Farragalli	666	(256, 203, 207)
3.	Eddie Lubanski	659	(227, 216, 216)
4.	Walter Ward	657	(245, 207, 205)
5.	Ray Bluth	653	(214, 237, 202)
6.	Earl Anthony	649	(194, 238, 217)
7.	Bill Lillard	641	(237, 217, 187)
8.	Andy Viripapa	623	(217, 206, 200)
9.	Steve Nagy	619	(197, 226, 196)
10.	Bob Strampe	616	(210, 203, 203)
11.	Dick Weber	613	(208, 215, 190)

The All-Time Bowling Tournament went to everyone's all-star, Don Carter. Surprisingly, two other popular T.V. bowlers, Earl Anthony (sixth) and Dick Weber (eleventh), did not do so well. Walter Ward held up the reputation of 1930's bowlers by taking fourth.

The big average bowlers seemed to maintain their consistency in this all-time tourney. However, there was some shifting around in their positions. The top average bowler, Carter, won the title. Lubanski, with the second best average, fell to third. Ward, with the third best average, fell to fourth.

Perhaps the big surprise of the tourney was Lindy Farragalli of the fifties, who took the lead in game one with the fourth best pre-tourney average. His score of 256 was the best of the entire tournament and enabled him to hold onto second place.

But the big news of the tournament was the consistency of Carter's game. He won by twenty-three pins, and showed that he deserves all the accolades he has received. In the common man's game, Don Carter is an uncommon master.

The All-Time Golf Tournament

The Field

The top ten golfers of all-time are set to tee off. To qualify, each golfer had to win five major tournaments. Here is a preview of the field, rated to play as they did in their peaks.

Walter Hagen (1892-1969) "The Haig," 5'10½", 185

Walter Hagen was the first giant of American golf. When he began competing, golf pros were often refused entrance into clubhouses and treated as second class citizens. With great shot-making and a colorful personality, he grabbed the public's attention and made pro golfers acceptable. He often said he was the first pro golfer to win a million and spend two.

He won four British Opens (in 1922, '24, '28, '29), two USGA Opens (1914 and '19), and a record five PGA's in 1921, '24, '25, '26, '27. His eleven major wins put him third on the all-time list behind Nicklaus and Jones. In an unofficial world championship match in Florida in 1926, Hagen handed Jones his worst defeat, 12 and 11.

Using a wide stance and a less than classic sway, he would spray several bad shots during most rounds. Unaffected, he would make great recovery shots and putt well from middle distances. He was a great competitor and showman.

Bobby Jones (1902-1971) 5'8", 160

Bobby Jones played only as an amateur and had fewer tournament appearances than most golfers. It did not keep him from compiling an awe-inspiring career record. He was the only man to win the old Grand Slam of the USGA and British Opens and the USGA and British amateurs in one year, 1930. Beginning play in 1916 (at age 14), it was 1923 before he won. From that time through 1930, he won four USGA Opens (1923, '26, '29, and '30), five Amateurs (1924, '25, '27, '28, '30), three British Opens (1926, '27, '30) and one British Amateur (1930). He retired in 1930 when only 28 years old. His record of 13 major wins seemed unbeatable until Nicklaus came along.

Jones had a graceful swing, was a long driver, and excellent putter. In early retirement he designed the Masters Course for Augusta National. A spinal ailment confined him to a wheelchair and brought on his death.

Gene Sarazen (born 1902) 5'5½", 162

Sarazen was one of golf's great players with one of the longest careers. A former caddie from a poor family, he first won the USGA Open at age 20. He won two Opens in 1922 and '32, one British Open in 1932, three PGA's in 1922, '23, '33 and one Masters in 1935, for seven major wins.

In a long dry spell before coming back in 1932, Sarazen developed the sand wedge. He made perhaps the most famous shot in golfing history. It was the 485 yard par 5, 15th hole at the 1935 Masters. Craig Wood was in the clubhouse with an apparent win. Sarazen dropped in a double eagle two on a 220-yard four-wood shot. He parred out, tied Wood, and beat him by five strokes in a playoff. He was easy to find for he always wore knickers.

Sam Snead (born 1912) 5'11", 185. "Slammin' Sammy"

The man with the perfect swing probably has had the longest successful career. He has won 84 assorted PGA tournaments and registered 134 total wins, both all-time records. His seven major wins include the Masters in 1949, '52, '54; the PGA in 1942, '49, '51; and the British Open in 1946. He won the Vardon Trophy for low average in 1938, '49, '50, '55, with his 1950 average of 69.23 still a record. He is co-holder of the PGA scoring records of 60 for 18 holes and 126 for 36 holes. He is well known for his straw hat and his poor putting.

Ben Hogan (born 1912) 5'8½", 145. "Bantam Ben"

A determined, tireless, machine-like veteran, he won nine major tournaments and came close several other times. He lost the Masters in a playoff with Byron Nelson in 1941. During World War II, Hogan was in the Navy and lost several playing years. Returning after the service, he won the PGA in 1946 and '48 and the Open in 1948. In 1949, he suffered a near-fatal car accident in Texas that left him with a broken pelvis and collarbone, ankle and ribs. Again he returned to win the Open in 1950, '51 and '53. He won the Masters in 1951 and '53 and the British Open in 1953 for three-fourths of the Grand Slam in that year. Many remember him limping with pain and visibly exhausted in these 1953 tournaments. Hogan also lost playoffs to Snead in the 1954 Masters and to Jack Fleck in the 1955 Open. In both the 1946 Open and Masters, he three-putted the last green to miss a playoff. He won three Vardon best-average trophies in 1940, '41 and '48. His Hale Open victory in 1942 was, in all but name, a U.S. Open win. With a little luck, he would have been no worse than the third greatest winner of major tournaments, but, instead, his nine wins put him fourth on the all-time list.

Byron Nelson (born 1912) 6'1", 179

Nelson was the top golfer of the late 1930's and 1940's. He won the USGA Open in 1939, the PGA in 1940, '45 and the Masters in 1937, '42 for five major wins. He won the Vardon Trophy in 1939 and also averaged 68.33 in 1945 when no Vardon Trophy was awarded. In that year, his only full year on the tour, he won eighteen times with eleven straight. Both 1945 scores are still records. His achievement has been questioned because such players as Hogan were in the war and not competing. As a hemophiliac, Nelson stayed

home and shot great scores against meager competition.
Shooting no four round totals over par in 1945, he showed he
was beating the courses as well as the opponents. After 1945
he retired to later become a T.V. commentator and golf
writer.

Arnold Palmer (born 1929) 5'11", 185

Palmer learned golf at age three from his dad and had one
of the most phenomenal and popular careers in the history of
golf. He ended his amateur career winning the USGA
Amateur in 1954. He made his mark on the game with a bold,
charging game, accompanied by "Arnie's Army" of de-
voted fans. In the 1960 USGA Open, he made up seven
strokes on Mike Souchak in the final round. He birdied six of
the first seven holes and shot 65 for the win. Other major
wins were the Masters in 1958, '60, '62 and the British Open
in 1961 and '62 for seven major wins. His 61 U.S. wins put
him third behind Snead and Hogan in that department. He
also won the Vardon Trophy for low average in 1961, '62,
'64 and '67. In recent years his game has declined, but not his
popularity.

Gary Player (born 1936) 5'8", 159

A South African, Player has traveled widely and won
tournaments all over the world. His eight major wins are the
USGA Open in 1965, the Masters in 1961, '74, '78, the
British Open in 1959, '68, '74 and the PGA in 1962. A
natural athlete, he jogs, lifts weights and eats natural foods.
He usually dresses in black. Often protested by those oppos-
ing South Africa's apartheid policy, Player always has been a
humanitarian. He introduced black Lee Elder to South African play.

Lee Trevino (born 1939) 5'7", 180

Trevino played and hustled in Texas to raise money to try
the PGA tour in 1967. He won the 1968 USGA Open for his
first victory. Talkative and friendly, he drew a big gallery
known as "Lee's Fleas" and became one of the tour's most

colorful players and biggest money winners. He beat Jack
Nicklaus in a playoff for the 1971 USGA Open. Other major
wins were the 1971 and '72 British Opens and the 1974 PGA,
for five major wins. He won three Vardon best average
trophies in 1970, '71 and '73. One of five golfers who are
million dollar winners, he is active in charity events and
plays in most of the tours.

Jack Nicklaus (born 1940) 5'11¾", 185, "The Golden
Bear"

One of the greatest golfers of all time, Nicklaus took up
golf at age 10 and won the USGA Amateur in 1959. He is the
all-time money winner and all-time major tournament winner, having broken Bobby Jones' seemingly unbeatable record. Through 1980 his nineteen major wins include the
USGA Amateur in 1959 and '61, five Masters (1963, '65,
'66, '72, '75), four USGA Opens (1962, '67, '72, '80), three
British Opens (1966, '70, '78) and five PGA's (1963, '71,
'73, '75, '80).

Nicklaus is still setting records, and will eventually trail
only Snead and Hogan in total U.S. tourney wins. He is the
only player to win all four major events twice. A money
player, Nicklaus aims for the big events, using a few others
as tune-ups. Nicklaus has become more popular after losing
weight and letting his hair grow. He has become a course
architect in recent years, with his favorite design being the
site of his own tournament, Muirfield Village Golf Club in
Dublin, Ohio.

The ten best golfers on eighteen of the best holes—what a
thrill! Who would win? The obvious favorites are the big
major tournament winners—Nicklaus (16), Jones (13),
Hagen (11) and Hogan (9). But judging by total U.S. wins,
Snead (84) and Hogan (unknown) outdistance Nicklaus (58
and still counting), Palmer (61) and Hagen (60). Judging by
stroke average, the leaders are Snead with four Vardon
Trophies and the record 69.23 in 1950, Palmer (4), Hogan

(3), Trevino (3) and Nelson (1). However, there were no Vardon Trophies and records were not as complete when Hagen and Jones played. If we judge by golf's premier prize, the attention swings to Bobby Jones, for he was the only golfer to win the Grand Slam. But that was the old version which counted the British and American amateur tournaments. No one has won the modern Grand Slam, although Jack Nicklaus has won each leg of it twice—the one golfer to do so.

If the all-time best golfers were being judged by a long series of matches, perhaps the scale would be tipped in favor of Snead and Hogan, with Palmer and Trevino in close pursuit. But this all-time tournament is one big event of four rounds. Therefore Nicklaus, Jones and Hagen look like the favorites for the biggest golf tournament ever.

One final statistic that is often overlooked is the record score in the major tournaments. Of the four tournaments in the Modern Grand Slam, Nicklaus shares the record for one of them. He and Ray Floyd both have a 271 (17 under) for the Masters and he possesses a similar record 271 for the U.S. Open. In addition, Nicklaus holds the USGA Amateur record at 282 and the U.S. Open record for an amateur at 282. Bobby Jones holds the amateur record for the British Open at 285. Nicklaus should be considered the favorite of this all-time tournament with four records in major tournaments to one for Jones. Nicklaus' record of 17 under for the major tournaments would be equivalent to a 263 on this course. That is the standard these all-time greats will shoot for.

The golfers are set to tee off on a mythical composite course of eighteen of the best holes in the United States. Who is your pick?

The Tournament

First Round   Par 70

Nicklaus	64	Par Out	533 445 443-35
Jones	65		

Hagen	66	Nicklaus	523 345 343-32
Palmer	66	Jones	524 445 333-33
Trevino	66		
Snead	66		
Hogan	69	Par In	534 434 543-35-70
Player	69		
Nelson	70	Nicklaus	443 334 534-32-64
Sarazen	70	Jones	434 433 434-32-65

The world's best golfers tore into the playoff course in the first round and left it embarrassed. No one was over par. The deepest marks were left by the "Golden Bear," Jack Nicklaus, who came in six under, edging out the little Georgian, Bobby Jones, for the lead. Hagen, Palmer, Trevino, and Snead all stayed close at four under.

Nicklaus and Jones went to work on the second hole, dropping birdie putts on the easy par three. Jones fell back on three, hitting the fairway trap and taking his only bogey. Nicklaus' two iron left him a three feet birdie putt on four. On seven, Jones putted from five feet and Nicklaus from 10, as both birdied. Jones went to two under and one back on eight after a good seven iron and a five feet birdie putt.

Both wedged on and dropped short birdie putts on the par five tenth hole. Jack got great approach shots at twelve and thirteen, dropping two four feet putts to go six under. After thirteen, Jones trailed by three. Nicklaus parred out from there on, but Jones wasn't through. A great five iron and a nine feet putt gave Jones a birdie at 15. On the par five sixteenth hole, Nicklaus was in two, but three-putted. Jones wedged on from twenty-five yards and dropped a bird from four feet.

Nicklaus at 64 and Jones at 65 had the best of several great rounds.

Second Round   Par 140

Nicklaus	64-64-128	Par Out	533 445 443-35
Hagen	66-64-130		

Jones	65-65-130	Nicklaus	433 445 432-32
Trevino	66-66-132	Hagen	433 455 433-34
Hogan	69-64-133	Jones	433 444 433-32
Snead	66-68-134	Hogan	423 345 442-31
Palmer	66-70-136		
Nelson	70-66-136		
Sarazen	70-67-137	Par In	534 434 534-35-70
Player	69-72-141		
		Nicklaus	434 324 534-32-64
		Hagen	433 334 433-30-64
		Jones	534 334 533-33-65
		Hogan	534 433 524-33-64

Nicklaus started the day with a one stroke lead over Jones and two strokes over four others. All the leaders began by birdying the par five first. None broke par until the sixth, when Jones wedged on and dropped a thirteen feet putt to draw even with Nicklaus. On the eight, Jones and Hagen birdied with short putts, but Nicklaus birdied in on a chip from five yards off the green. Nicklaus again took the lead by dropping a 19-foot putt on the difficult par three ninth hole.

The back nine opened with Nicklaus and Hagen birdying hole ten. At this point, Nicklaus led Jones by two and Hagen by four. Hagen began a charge by birdying number 12. Nicklaus, Hagen and Jones all birdied 13. At 14, Nicklaus dropped a five feet birdie to go up three on Jones and four on Hagen. Hagen birdied sixteen, and both Hagen and Jones birdied eighteen to bring the two back to two strokes down.

Another brilliant 64 by Hogan moved him into fifth, but it was somewhat obscured as the three leaders fought it out. Trevino shot his second 66 to take fourth, four strokes back. But Nicklaus' two 64's was holding off all challenges.

Third Round   Par 210

Nicklaus	64-64-67-195	Par Out	533 445 443-35
Hogan	69-64-63-196		
Hagen	66-64-67-197	Nicklaus	523 445 452-34

Jones	65-65-67-197	Hagen	523 445 343-33
Trevino	66-66-67-199	Jones	424 435 344-33
Snead	66-68-66-200	Hogan	523 335 443-32
Palmer	66-70-66-202		
Sarazen	70-67-67-204		
Nelson	70-66-69-205	Par In	534 434 534-35-70
Player	69-72-65-206		
		Nicklaus	434 435 424-33-67
		Hagen	435 434 434-34-67
		Jones	544 435 433-34-67
		Hogan	433 334 524-31-63

The course began to assert itself in round three. The leaders all faltered. Jones was all over the course and Nicklaus briefly lost the lead on the eighth hole. When the sand had settled in the traps, only two strokes separated the first four.

The day belonged to Hogan, who astounded with a 63 and surged into second place. He actually tied for the lead after fifteen holes.

Nicklaus hit five roughs and three traps, but putted well for five birdies and two bogies. The usually steady Jones hit eight roughs, one trap, and the water on hole 11 on his way to seven birdies and four bogies. Hagen was more consistent with only one bogey, but Hogan was hot with approaches so accurate that putting seemed unnecessary.

When the golfers came to the eighth hole for the day, Jones and Hogan were three under par, Hagen two under, and Nicklaus but one under. Nicklaus chipped on in three and two-putted from seven feet for a bogey. Jones went into the lead. Nicklaus and Hagen were one back, and Hogan three back. On the ninth, Nicklaus birdied while Jones bogied. Jones and Hagen fell one back and went on to finish eighteen holes behind by two.

Meanwhile, Hogan put together three quick birdies on the back nine. When Nicklaus blasted from a sand trap on 15, he two-putted from forty-five feet for a bogey. This left him tied with Hagen for the lead. But Jack rallied with two birdies on 16 and 17 and held off Hogan's charge by one stroke. Hagen and Jones held at two back.

Final Round   Par 280

Nicklaus	64-64-67-69-264	Par Out	533	445	443-35
Hagen	66-64-67-68-265				
Jones	65-65-67-68-265	Nicklaus	533	445	443-35
Hogan	69-64-63-70-266	Hogan	523	435	543-34
Snead	66-68-66-67-267	Hagen	523	354	344-33
Palmer	66-70-66-66-268	Jones	533	445	444-36
Trevino	66-66-67-70-269				
Nelson	70-66-69-66-271				
Player	69-72-65-70-274	Par In	534	434	534-35-7•
Sarazen	70-67-67-71-275				
		Nicklaus	435	334	435-34-6•
		Hogan	434	524	635-36-7•
		Hagen	433	444	454-35-6:
		Jones	434	434	424-32-6:

Today, in the thrilling final round of the all-time golf tournament, Jack Nicklaus emerged as the winner. Nicklaus began the day with a one stroke lead. Before it was over, both Hogan and Hagen would steal the lead only to lose it again. Jones never led, but closed to within one stroke on the final hole.

The day began with Hogan continuing his streak of the previous day. Both he and Hagen dropped birdie putts from about fifteen feet on the second hole. Hogan had drawn even with Nicklaus and Hagen was just one back. On the par four fourth hole, Hagen dropped a 16-foot putt, and it was a three way tie with Jones two strokes back. On the remaining fourteen holes, the leaders rose and fell so often that the excitement was almost unbearable.

On the difficult fifth hole, Hagen hit a trap and bogied. Hogan birdied from eleven feet to take the lead as his streak continued. Jones and Nicklaus continued to par each hole. Hagen came back to birdie the par five sixth, dropping a bending 37-foot putt.

The seventh hole was pivotal. Hogan hit the left rough, then the trap, and bogied. Hagen rolled in a 30-foot putt and took the lead, with Hogan and Nicklaus one back. Hagen then fell in the trees about 175 yards out on number nine. His nine iron rolled over the green to a trap, giving him a bogey. Jones two-putted from five feet for his first bogey. The front nine ended in a three-way tie, with Jones falling three back.

The four leaders all birdied the par five tenth hole and parred the eleventh. On the twelfth hole, Nicklaus went in the ocean and took a bogey. Hagen hit the green and rolled in a 13-footer for a bird, a stroke lead over Hogan and two over Nicklaus.

On the tight fairways of hole 13, Hogan hit the trees and bogied, while Nicklaus birdied. Hagen was still on top, with Nicklaus one back, Hogan two back, and Jones three back.

On the par three fourteenth hole, Hagen hit the trees and bogied, while Hogan rolled in a five footer for a bird. Again it was a three-way tie, with Jones remaining three back.

The leaders all parred 15. Hogan bogied the par five sixteenth hole to fall out of contention while the other leaders all got birdies. With two holes to go, Nicklaus and Hagen were tied, Hogan was two back, and Jones three back.

With the title on the line, the aggressive play of the charging Hagen cost him a possible win. A hooked two wood landed in the ocean and Hagen took a double bogie on the par three seventeenth hole. Jones moved a stroke closer with a birdie. Hagen had taken himself out of it. Now, Nicklaus had a two stroke lead over the other three with just one hole to go.

The leaders all missed the green on the par four eighteenth hole. All on in three, Jones was four feet away, Hagen six, Nicklaus three, and Hogan eight. Surprisingly, Nicklaus missed, but took a bogey and a one stroke win. Hagen and

Jones with pars finished tied, just one stroke back. Hogan also bogied to finish two back. Farther back, Snead with a 67 and Palmer with his third 66, moved past Trevino in the standings. Nelson, Player, and Sarazen finished out the field. Every golfer in the tournament shot under par.

Jack Nicklaus, the big tournament player, won the all-time golf tournament with a 16 under 264. It was just one under his 17 under record pace for both the Masters and U.S. Open. Despite his great score, the competition was fierce and his win was certainly not as dominating as many would have expected. In retrospect, it was probably Hagen's hard charging play that presented even more of a challenge than Jones' consistency. Indeed, if Hagen could have parred at 17 instead of collecting that double bogey, he would have pulled off the upset.

Finally, after all the "what ifs," Nicklaus reigns supreme. It was a close, but deserved win, and he showed that he could deliver when necessary.

The All-Time Thoroughbred Horse Race

The Field

The all-time horse race will pit the best three-year-olds against each other over a fast mile-and-a-quarter track. The field was chosen from the top three-year-olds and the best handicap horses. Most sports fans know that the Triple Crown for three-year-olds (Kentucky Derby, Preakness, and Belmont Stakes) is one measure of supremacy in the racing world. Through 1979, there have been eleven Triple Crown winners. Two of them, Citation and Secretariat, are in this all-time field. Many other horses have won two races of the famed Triple Crown. From that group, Man o' War, Nashua, and Damascus made the all-time field. One horse, Buck-passer, qualified as a three-year-old even though he won none of the Triple Crown races. The other five entries in the field are the eminent handicap horses of all-time: Swaps, Roundtable, Kelso, Dr. Fager, and Forego.

Here is a preview of the field of all-time thoroughbred horses, rated for performance at the best year of their careers:

Man o' War—3 year old, 1920

"Big Red" was voted the greatest horse of the half-century by the Associated Press in 1950. As a three year old, he won all eleven races he entered. After not entering the Kentucky Derby in 1920, Man o' War won the final two legs of the Triple Crown. He set five American track records during that same year. His near-perfect career record shows 20 wins and one second in 21 starts. Man o' War's only loss was dealt to him by a horse named, ironically, Upset.

A chestnut colt, Man o' War is the son of Fair Play and Mahubah. He will be ridden by Clarence Kummer, his usual rider.

Citation—3 year old, 1948

The eighth Triple Crown winner, Citation won 27 of 29 races as a two- and three-year-old. He was the first horse to accumulate total earnings of a million dollars. Citation's career record was 32 wins, 10 seconds and two thirds in 45 starts.

A bay colt, Citation is the son of Bull Lea and Hydroplane II. Up in the saddle will be his regular rider, Eddie Arcaro, the third winningest jockey of all-time.

Nashua—3 year old, 1955

After losing to Swaps in the 1955 Kentucky Derby, Nashua went on to win the remaining two legs of the Triple Crown. He later renewed his rivalry with Swaps, beating the latter in a special match race at Washington Park. His career record reveals 22 wins, four seconds and one third in 30 starts.

The brown colt was sired by Nasrullah out of Segula. He will be ridden by Ted Atkinson, with his usual rider, Eddie Arcaro, opting for Citation.

Swaps–4 year old, 1956

In 1955, Swaps recorded a win and a loss in competition with Nashua. Swaps was even more impressive as a four-year-old, setting four world records. Injuries forced his retirement after his fourth racing season. His career record was 19 wins, two seconds and two thirds in 25 starts.

A chestnut colt, Swaps is the son of Khaled and Iron Reward. The rider will be his favorite, Johnny Longden, the second all-time winner among jockeys.

Roundtable—4 year old, 1958

A great handicap horse, Roundtable was out of the money only six times between ages three to five. He set or equaled eleven track records while registering 43 wins, eight seconds and five thirds in 66 career starts.

A bay colt, son of Princequillo and Knight's Daughter, Roundtable's rider will be his regular jockey, Bill Hartack.

Kelso—6 year old, 1963

One of two six-year-olds in the field, Kelso actually raced until he was nine. Five times "Horse of the Year," Kelso's $1,977,896 total career winnings top the all-time money list. He also holds the American two mile record. Kelso had 39 wins, 12 seconds and two thirds in 63 starts.

A dark bay gelding, Kelso is son of Your Host and Maid of Flight. He will be ridden by Ishmael Valenzuela.

Buckpasser—3 year old, 1966

Although he failed to win any of the Triple Crown events, Buckpasser once won 15 straight races. A pressure horse, his career record shows 25 wins, four seconds and one third in 31 starts.

The bay colt is the son of Tom Fool and Busanda. Buckpasser will be ridden by Walter Blum, the fifth all-time winningest jockey.

Damascus—3 year old, 1967

Damascus established a sensational record as a three-year-old. After finishing third in the Kentucky Derby, he proceeded to win both the Preakness and Belmont Stakes. He went on to defeat Buckpasser and Dr. Fager, two of his earlier opponents, in the memorable 1967 Woodward Stakes. His career record was 21 wins, seven seconds and three thirds in 32 starts.

A bay colt, he is the son of Sword Dancer and Kerala. Damascus has up in the saddle the all-time winningest jockey, Willie Shoemaker.

Dr. Fager—4 year old, 1968

As a four-year-old, Dr. Fager won seven of eight races while carrying heavy weights. A speed horse, his limit was

1¼ miles. Dr. Fager holds the world's mile record at 1:32$^{1}/_{5}$, and is considered the premier sprinter in racing history. He posted 18 wins, two seconds and one third in 22 career starts.

A bay colt, Dr. Fager is the son of Rough 'n Tumble and Aspidistra. His rider will be Braulio Baeza, the top money winner for the four-year period 1965 to 1968.

Secretariat—3 year old, 1973

The modern "super horse" of Man o' War's class, Secretariat was the ninth Triple Crown winner. He was voted "Horse of the Year" as both a two- and three-year-old. Secretariat holds both the Kentucky Derby and Belmont Stakes records. No horse has come within two seconds of his 2:24 time over the Belmont's long 1½ mile course. Secretariat also shares the world record for the 1⅛ distance. He was syndicated for breeding at a record price of six million dollars after his third year of racing. His short career ended with 16 wins, three seconds and one third in 21 starts.

A big chestnut colt, Secretariat is the son of Bold Ruler and Something Royal. He is ridden by his "number one fan," Ron Turcotte.

Forego—6 year old, 1976

Forego's three "Horse of the Year" awards were topped only by Kelso's five similar honors. Forego is also runner-up to Kelso in total career earnings. In his sixth year, Forego registered six wins, one second and one third in eight starts. His career record was 34 wins, nine seconds and seven thirds in 57 starts.

A bay gelding, Forego is the son of Forli and Lady Golconda. He will be ridden by Lafitte Pincay, the top money winning jockey from 1970 to 1974.

There are some definite surprises in the field, most notably the sprint horse, Dr. Fager, who has rarely been put in this class of horses by sportswriters. The omission of such greats as Seabiscuit, War Admiral, Tom Fool, Native Dancer, and Whirlaway may also raise a few eyebrows. After careful evaluation, however, these horses were judged to be a grade below the final eleven entries.

There is no clear-cut favorite in the field. Although they are racing at the Kentucky Derby distance of 1¼ miles, only three of the entries—Citation, Swaps, and Secretariat—ever won that event. The race is being held at Hollywood Park, California, a very fast track. Swaps raced there quite frequently, but most of the other horses never even saw the track. Each horse is carrying 126 pounds, a possible advantage for the handicap horses who often carried much more weight.

In attempting to determine the greatest horse of all-time, sports observers have pointed to a wide variety of performance indicators. The most frequently quoted statistics are career win percentages, total earnings, records set, and best single year.

Judging on the percentage of wins in a career, Man o' War (95%), Dr. Fager (82%), and Buckpasser (81%) are the class of the field. The short careers of Man o' War and Dr. Fager, however, call into question their high percentages.

Using total earnings as the criterion of supremacy, the top three all-time career money winners—Kelso, Forego, and Roundtable—should be considered the best. However, each of these three horses had twice as many starts as the fifth all-time money-winner, Buckpasser, making their accomplishment look less impressive. If the standard of excellence is most money won in a horse's best single year, then Secretariat ($860,404), Damascus ($817,941), and Nashua ($752,550) are the leaders.

If judging the best horse of all time by records set for speed, then Dr. Fager and Secretariat are the top choices. Dr. Fager holds the world one mile record; Secretariat shares the world 1⅛ mile mark. No other entry can lay claim to a world record. Secretariat holds two of the three Triple Crown records, including the Kentucky Derby mark of 1:59²/₅ over

1¼ miles—the distance of the all-time horse race. However, Swaps and Roundtable each ran a faster time of 1:58³/₅ over this same distance in the Hollywood Gold Cup (no longer a record). Several other horses have record-setting potential.

For our purposes, horses have been evaluated on the basis of their best, or peak, year. The number of races in an entry's peak year varies from a low of eight for Forego and Dr. Fager to a high of twenty for Citation. Judging on the percentage of races won during their peak year, Man o' War (100%), Citation (95%), and Buckpasser (93%) head the field. Citation is particularly impressive with 19 wins and one second in 20 starts.

Have you made your pick? Here is a final look at the horses as they go to the post. The odds have been set on the basis of the horses' overall records and reputations. They will run, however, only on the record they compiled during their peak year.

Post Position	Horse	Jockey	Odds
1	Man o' War	C. Kummer	2½-1
2	Swaps	J. Longden	4-1
3	Dr. Fager	B. Baeza	4½-1
4	Secretariat	R. Turcotte	3-1
5	Citation	E. Arcaro	4-1
6	Buckpasser	W. Blum	4-1
7	Damascus	W. Shoemaker	8½-1
8	Roundtable	B. Hartack	6-1
9	Forego	L. Pincay	6-1
10	Kelso	I. Valenzuela	8½-1
11	Nashua	T. Atkinson	6-1

Ages: 3 year olds and up
Distance: 1¼ miles
The Track: Hollywood Park, California
Condition of the Track: Fast
Track Record: 1:58¹/₅ by Quack

The Race

Man o' War broke quickly on top by a length, followed by Dr. Fager, Swaps, and Nashua. Citation and Roundtable tucked in behind. Secretariat ran two lengths back. Kelso, Forego, Buckpasser, and Damascus trailed. The horses held their positions as they sped around the turn.

At the half-mile, Citation pulled up even with Man o' War, Dr. Fager, Swaps, and Nashua in a five-way tie for the lead. Roundtable, Secretariat, and the field followed.

As they moved past the three-quarter pole, Dr. Fager's speed put him in the lead by two lengths. Secretariat and Buckpasser charged forward and dueled for second. Man o' War, Citation, and Swaps were two lengths in back of the three leaders. The rest of the field trailed.

At the one-mile mark, Secretariat took the lead by two lengths. Man o' War slipped into second place, a head past Buckpasser and Dr. Fager. A length back were Citation and Swaps, who opened up a three-length margin over the others.

At the head of the stretch, it was Secretariat who continued to lead. Man o' War pulled within a length to second. Buckpasser was another length back in third. Dr. Fager, Citation, and Swaps battled each other for fourth place.

In the stretch drive, Secretariat and Man o' War pulled away from the field. With a hard-driving charge, Secretariat outran Man o' War to win by two lengths. Man o' War hit the finish line three full lengths ahead of Buckpasser, who held off Dr. Fager by a length. Citation and Swaps finished in a dead heat for fifth. Damascus crossed the wire in seventh place. Roundtable and Forego tied for eighth. Nashua and Kelso trailed.

Secretariat's winning time of 1:58 established a new track record at Hollywood Park. Presented below is a list of the horses in their order of finish:

Results of the All-Time Thoroughbred Horse Race

1. Secretariat
2. Man o' War
3. Buckpasser
4. Dr. Fager
5. Citation (tie)
5. Swaps (tie)
7. Damascus
8. Roundtable (tie)
8. Forego (tie)
10. Nashua
11. Kelso

Time: 1:58.0 New track record for mile and a quarter
Win: Secretariat $8.00, $3.80, $2.60
Place: Man o' War $3.60, $2.40
Show: Buckpasser $2.80

The two "super horses," Secretariat and Man o' War, lived up to their reputations in an exciting race dominated by the three-year-olds. But it was Secretariat, with Ron Turcotte in the saddle, who finished with a driving charge to establish himself as the greatest thoroughbred racehorse of all-time.

The All-Time 100-Meter Freestyle (Swimming)

The Field

Who is the fastest swimmer in history? The glamour boys of water sports will compete over 100 meters for the all-time freestyle swimming title. Aside from being beautiful physical specimens, the swimmers are remarkable athletes. Each entrant in the all-time field once held the record in this event. Here is a historical preview of the select field:

Entry and Country	Number of AAU Titles	Olympic Gold Medal Year	Best Time
John Weismuller, U.S.	4	1924, 1928	57.8
Jon Henricks, Australia	None	1956	55.4
Don Schollander, U.S.	3	1964	53.4
Mike Wenden, Australia	None	1968	52.2
Mark Spitz, U.S.	3	1972	51.22
Jim Montgomery, U.S.	1	1976	49.99
Jonty Skinner, S. Africa	2	None	49.44

The field for the All-Time 100-Meter Freestyle presents some unusual contrasts. John Weismuller became an international celebrity for his portrayal of Tarzan in the classic movie series. All of the other entrants, with the possible exception of Mark Spitz, are virtually unknown outside the world of swimming. Some of the swimmers are known principally for their performances in the 100-meter freestyle while others competed at longer distances. A few even tried different strokes.

The field crosses three time periods. Weismuller represents the twenties with his duel Olympic gold medal victories in 1924 and 1928. Jon Henricks of Australia offers the best of the fifties' swimmers. The rest of the field competed from 1964 through the present day.

The obvious standouts in the all-time field are Weismuller, Don Schollander, and Mark Spitz. Weismuller won five gold medals in two Olympiads. Three of his medals came in 1924—in the 100-meters, 400-meters, and 800-meter relay. He set 24 world records and was said to have never lost a race between 50 and 880 yards in ten years of competition.

In 1964, Don Schollander became the first swimmer to win four gold medals in a single Olympiad. He was the first athlete to accomplish this feat since Jesse Owens' track victories at the 1936 Olympics. His freestyle victories in the 100-meters, 400-meters, 400-meter relay, and 880-meter relay all set Olympic records. He broke a world record in all but the 100-meter event.

In 1968, Mark Spitz predicted he would win six Olympic gold medals. He managed to take home only two, both in team events. In 1972, at twenty-two years of age, Spitz returned to the Olympics. This time, however, he made no predictions. He simply competed in seven events, winning all seven in world record times! Four of his medals were won in freestyle events—the 100-meters, 200-meters, 400-meter relay, and 800-meter relay. His other wins came in the 100-meter butterfly, 200-meter butterfly, and the butterfly leg of the 400-meter medley relay. It should be noted that four of Spitz's victories scored in newly-added events, thus serving to inflate his medals total.

Of the remaining entrants in the all-time field, Australian Mike Wenden scored a double gold medal victory in the 100- and 200-meter freestyle events in 1968. Jim Montgomery won the 100-meters in 1976, but failed in his bid to capture the 200-meters. Jonty Skinner, the most recent record-holder in the 100-meter freestyle, usually lost to Montgomery in this event. The other Australian in the field, Jon Henricks, turned in a sensational time of 55.4 in the 100-meters back in the 1956 Olympics.

It is very likely that Jonty Skinner's world record mark of 49.44 will be broken in the All-Time 100-Meter Freestyle. Throughout history, past records in this event were constantly bettered. Of the seventeen times the modern Olympics have been held, the 100-meter freestyle record has been eclipsed fifteen times!

The favorites in the race appear to be the Olympians who garnered the most gold medals. However, the top medal winner, Mark Spitz, is better known for the butterfly than his freestyle. Schollander broke three world records in the Olympics, but failed to break the mark in the 100-meters. Weismuller was unbeatable in the twenties, but it is questionable whether he will hold up against the modern swimmers. Montgomery and Skinner have traded victories in recent years. The Aussies' Mike Wenden performed well in a single Olympiad and his fellow countryman, Jon Henricks, is best known for his fast time in this single event during the 1956 Games. Between the famous Americans, the lesser known Australians, and the modern South African, it's anybody's race. Who do you pick to win?

The Race

Montgomery and Skinner got off to a quick start and held the lead through most of the first lap. Spitz, Henricks, and Schollander closed quickly on Montgomery and Skinner at the turn. Schollander and Henricks came out of the turn with the lead. Both men swam hard as they led the field down the stretch. Montgomery held firm in third place. Wenden kicked past Spitz with about twenty-five meters to go. Skinner fell back with Weismuller. It was Schollander and Henricks in a virtual dead heat as they approached the wall. The two leaders touched on the same stroke, with Henricks getting the win by three one-hundredths of a second. Montgomery finished a half-length back in third, an arm up on Wenden. Spitz narrowly edged out Skinner, who held off the fast-closing Weismuller to avoid finishing last.

Presented below is the final order of finish in the All-Time 100-Meter Freestyle:

1. Jon Henricks   47.81 (World Record)
2. Don Schollander   47.84
3. Jim Montgomery   48.26
4. Mike Wenden   48.34
5. Mark Spitz   48.52
6. Jonty Skinner   48.84
7. John Weismuller   49.11

In a thrilling race, Henricks of the 1950's and Schollander of the mid-sixties proved to be the class of the field. The modern-day swimmers held fast in the middle of the pack and Weismuller, the old-timer, finished last. No entrant has anything to be ashamed of. All finished within 1.3 seconds of the leader and all broke the existing world record! Australia, with a second and a fourth, appeared to outduel, but not dominate, the Americans.

The All-Time 100-Meter Freestyle provided the biggest record-breaking performance in the entire Computer Sports Matchup series. And topping the list of record-breakers was Australian Jon Henricks, the fastest swimmer of all-time.

The All-Time Men's Tennis Tournament

The Field

Tournament tennis has a long history which began at historic Wimbledon in 1877. However, only after World War I, with the appearance of Bill Tilden and Suzanne Lenglen, did tennis achieve star status and become a spectator sport. Through the late 1930's, tournament tennis was primarily for amateurs, and the winners of the Wimbledon and United States lawn tournaments were considered the world's best. From the 1940's through the 1960's, professional tennis grew. With the pros excluded from the most prestigious tournaments, it became difficult to determine who were the best players. In 1968, open play returned, and amateurs and professionals could compete together.

For purposes of this All-Time Tournament, players were chosen on the basis of their performance in the historic major United States and Wimbledon lawn tournaments. Here is a preview of the eight great male stars who will contend for the all-time title.

Bill Tilden. The first superstar of men's tennis, this American won three Wimbledon and six United States singles titles between 1920 and '30. Tilden boasts a win streak of thirteen Davis Cup singles matches. He had a big serve and much endurance. However, his style of staying solely on the baseline might be threatened by more aggressive later players and might damage his chance of becoming the all-time best.

Jean-René LaCoste. France's best player, he won two

Wimbledon, two United States, and three French singles titles during the 1924-29 period. Exclusively a baseline defensive player, he used lobs and controlled groundstrokes well. He was the last great player to favor the baseline over the volley approach.

Fred Perry. England's best player, he won three Wimbledon, three United States, one Australian, and one French singles titles during 1931-36. He was the first player to win all four of the Grand Slam Tournaments, although he did not do it in one year. His style featured speed and a running forehand. He was good in big matches, but weak in practicing.

Don Budge. This American had a brilliant but short amateur career, winning two Wimbledon, two United States, one Australian, and one French title during 1935-38. In 1938, he became the first amateur to win the Grand Slam and then became a successful professional. Showing no apparent weaknesses, he had a big serve and an attacking rolled backhand. Add his height and an excellent service return to these characteristics and you have a complete player.

Jack Kramer. Winning one Wimbledon and two United States singles titles during 1940-47, this American was a professional success as both player and promoter. Fast, powerful and accurate, he was the foremost proponent of the "Big Game" of serve and volley. He helped create the concept of the best percentage shot.

"Pancho" Gonzalez. Known primarily for his big serve, this American won the United States singles tournaments in 1948 and 1949. He turned pro early and became dominant on the tour. He supplemented his serve with great endurance, as indicated by his 112 game record match with Charles Pasarell in 1969. A dynamic personality, he showed a weakness in ground stroke play.

Rod Laver. Australia's best, he won four Wimbledon, two

United States, three Australian, and two French singles titles between 1959 and 1970. He is the only double winner of the Grand Slam in 1962 and 1969. Laver's career was divided into three periods: amateur 1959-62, pro 1963-68, and open from 1969. In 1962 he won all six major tournaments he entered—a feat never done before. If not the best ever, he is certainly the best left-hander ever. Laver's game was complete in all facets when he was at his peak, in 1962.

Bjorn Borg. Sweden's best player was the first to win Wimbledon five straight (1976-80) since the challenge round had been eliminated in 1912. He also won four French titles (1974, '75, '78, '79). Originally better on clay, he added a serve and volley game to his offensive backcourt play. A right hander with a two-handed backhand, he rarely shows emotion or gets ruffled. He is tall and extremely mobile.

The following pairings have been made for the All-Time Men's Tennis Tournament.

> Bill Tilden vs. Jean-René LaCoste
> "Pancho" Gonzalez vs. Rod Laver
> Don Budge vs. Jack Kramer
> Fred Perry vs. Bjorn Borg

Who will win the All-Time Men's Tennis Tournament? The surface is the classic grass and will favor the big servers. Tilden, Budge, Kramer, and Gonzalez all have big serves. Budge and Kramer will square off in the first round. Tilden and Budge traditionally have been put at the top of any all-time list. But what about the strength of the only double Grand Slam winner, the southpaw Laver? LaCoste is the only purely defensive player. How will he fare against Tilden on grass? The United States has four entries. Will an outsider hit them a passing shot? Borg has the best Wimbledon record and they're playing on the grass. Will that make the difference? Who is your pick as the all-time best?

The Tournament

First Round: Bill Tilden over Jean-René LaCoste: 6-4, 3-6, 4-6, 7-5, 6-4

Bill Tilden tried out his offensive baseline game against the most defensive player in the tournament and came out the winner. Tilden's big serve took the first set, with a service break in game three. Tilden then seemed to relax, losing the second set and falling behind 1-5 in the third. He battled back, but lost the third set. He continued to fight in long rallies and took a hard fourth set and drew even. Tilden broke service in game one of the fifth set and coasted to victory. LaCoste's baseline play carried Tilden to five sets, but the victory was easier than the score indicated.

First Round: Rod Laver over "Pancho" Gonzalez: 5-7, 6-3, 3-6, 7-5, 6-4

The Rocket beat Pancho in a long, grueling match. Laver started slowly and lost the first set to the durable Gonzalez, who held on to win five deuce games. Laver came back in set two, but was overpowered in set three and fell behind again. Laver won set four in a grueling replay of the long first set. In set five, Laver broke service in the first game. Each game was bitterly fought and included long rallies. Although Gonzalez never did give up, Laver held on to win. Laver was tested but stood up to the challenge, showing a better total game.

First Round: Don Budge over Jack Kramer: 1-6, 6-4, 6-3, 6-4

Two sluggers came out to go for the knockout. Budge suffered a knockdown, but came back for the knockout win. Kramer won the first game at love. Budge lost his first two serves and the first set 1-6. From then on, Budge played serve and volley to perfection. He kept Kramer off balance with fine ground strokes, taking the next three sets and the victory.

First Round: Bjorn Borg over Fred Perry: 2-6, 6-4, 6-3, 4-6, 6-4

In a battle of two extremely mobile players, Borg seemed to play and get the win without too much effort. Perry started quickly and won 6-2 over a lethargic Borg. Borg then played mechanically and flawlessly for two sets, and went up 2-1. He seemed to relax in set four and lost it. In set five, Borg seemed to expend just a little more effort, breaking Perry's third service and coasting to the win.

Semifinal: Bill Tilden over Rod Laver: 6-4, 2-6, 4-6, 14-12, 9-7

A durable old-timer barely edged out a durable modern. Tilden again proved his mettle by taking an early lead, coasting, and then holding on. Trailing by a set, Tilden played his baseline game to perfection in set four. He held on to win over Laver, who did not weaken at all. After the grueling fourth set it seemed as if the stronger player would win. However, neither weakened, and they went into overtime again. Long rallies continued and Tilden held on to win 9-7 in a classic five set struggle with very little separating the two. The past had conquered the present.

Semifinal: Bjorn Borg over Don Budge: 6-3, 4-6, 10-8, 2-6, 6-4

In the battle of the backhanders, it was Borg breaking Budge. Borg got an early service break and took set one. Budge came back with strong overall play to even the match. Set three was 8-8, 30-40, when Budge double-faulted and Borg served for the set at 10-8. Borg seemed to let down, losing the fourth set 2-6. With the match on the line, Borg broke Budge's first service and held on to win.

Final: Bjorn Borg over Bill Tilden: 5-7, 6-4, 4-6, 12-10, 6-4

The final shaped up as a battle of endurance between two great baseline players. Tilden had to go to 7-5 to take the first set. But Borg came back 6-4 in the second. Tilden broke Borg, winning set three 6-4. It looked like Tilden's serve might make the difference. Borg refused to bend in an extended fourth set that was reminiscent of Tilden's 14-12 comeback against Laver. Leading 11-10, Borg broke Tilden at 15-40 as Tilden seemed to wilt. Borg stayed on top of Tilden in set five to take the all-time title 6-4. In the second of the two longest matches of the tournament, Tilden finally ran out of gas. Surviving after 70 games with Laver, he finally weakened in the 54th game of this match. Borg was best, but Tilden had held on tenaciously until the end.

Surprises of surprises! After years of tennis domination by Australia and the United States, a Swede sneaks up and wins the All-Time title. In winning the title, Borg did not display the overpowering serve that some of the others possessed. What he did exhibit was consistency and endurance. In beating Budge, Borg showed he could stand up to the best serve and volley play. His defeat of Tilden showed he could beat a master baseliner. He may not have been overwhelming, but he was better than the very best players in tennis history. We honor Bjorn Borg as the All-Time Best Grass Court Male Tennis Player.

The All-Time Women's Tennis Tournament

The Field

Tennis is one women's sport that has a long tradition and for which a good set of records has been kept. Women competed at Wimbledon just seven years after the men began. In 1887, women's tennis came to the United States Championships.

In this all-time tennis tournament, women from as far back as the 1920's will be competing for the title of the greatest in history. The eight finalists include some of the most sparkling performers in the last 60 years of women's tennis. Though unknown to much of the sports world, these stars had some of the most impressive records in all of sports. Here is a preview of the eight finalists who will contend for the All-Time Best Women's Grass Court Championship:

Suzanne Lenglen. Emerging after World War I as the first super star of tennis, this French great won six Wimbledon and three French singles titles. In the eight years between 1919-26, she lost only once when she had to retire due to an injury in the 1921 United States Championship. Temperamental in nature, she was a veritable ballerina on the court, soaring to reach all manner of shots. Not possessing a great serve, she nevertheless went to the net a lot and possessed great ball control. In 1926, at age 26, she beat the next great, 19-year-old Helen Wills 6-3, 8-6 at Cannes in their only meeting.

Helen (Wills) Moody. An American, she won eight Wimbledon, seven United States, and four French singles titles.

Her record of eight Wimbledon wins was accomplished in nine attempts. Boasting a record probably second only to Lenglen, she lost no sets between 1927 and '32. Called "Little Poker Face," she possessed a big serve and a hard, deep baseline game, but showed very little back-to-front court mobility.

Alice Marble. Coming immediately after Mrs. Moody, this American won one Wimbledon and four United States titles while active from 1933-39. Although a small woman, she was the first to play the "man's" serve-volley game. She hit for winners, but did not show consistent control. World War II interrupted her career.

Maureen Connolly (Mrs. N. Brinker). "Little Mo," an American, won three Wimbledon, three United States, one Australian and two French titles, peaking during 1952-54. In 1953, at age 19, she became the first woman to win the Grand Slam. She won her first U.S. Championship when but 16. When only 20, a riding accident ended her career. She was essentially a strong, deep, and accurate baseline player. She was a natural southpaw who switched over.

Althea Gibson (Mrs. W. Darbon). An American, and the first black to be successful in tennis, she won two Wimbledon, and two United States singles Championships, playing strongest from 1956-58. She turned pro early, ending her competition in major events. "Big Al" was tall and muscular and brought to women's tennis the volley and the athletic approach, developed further by Margaret Court.

Margaret (Smith) Court. Australia's greatest woman won three Wimbledon, five United States, eleven Australian and five French singles titles in the years 1961-73. She won the Grand Slam in 1970 and amassed 85 major titles. She had rare power and a strong volley game.

Billie Jean (Moffit) King. This American won six Wimbledon, four United States, one Australian, and one French singles titles in her peak years from 1962-73. An attacking player, she used speed, lobs, serve-volley, and low volley techniques. She pushed for equal money for women's tennis. In 1979 she broke the record for the most total Wimbledon titles.

Chris (Evert) Lloyd. This current American has won two Wimbledon, five United States, and two French singles titles in a career that began to peak in 1971. She is a strong baseline player who possesses a two-hand backhand of rare power and accuracy. She was nearly unbeatable on clay for several years.

The pairings for the Women's Tennis Tournament are as follows:

> Suzanne Lenglen vs. Alice Marble
> Maureen Connolly vs. Althea Gibson
> Helen Wills Moody vs. Margaret Smith Court
> Chris Evert vs. Billie Jean King

The All-Time Tennis Tournament is being held on grass, which should favor the strong Wimbledon players. The old-timers, Lenglen and Moody, were virtually unbeatable at Wimbledon, or anywhere, and should be considered the class of the tournament. However, the moderns were strong, too. King won six Wimbledons, and Connolly won three straight in basically a three year career.

Style matchups could be interesting with three baseline players—Moody, Connolly, and Evert—dueling five offensive-minded players. Moody and Court, two of the biggest servers, are matched in the first round. Who will win that slugfest? The United States has six entries. Will an outsider overcome their numerical dominance? Will the winner be a big server, a baseliner, an American or an old-timer? Who is your pick to win the all-time tournament?

The Tournament

First Round: Suzanne Lenglen over Alice Marble: 1-6, 6-4, 6-1

Lenglen's court acrobatics were matched against Marble's serve-and-volley in this match. Alice Marble kept Lenglen away from the net and swept to a 6-1 first set win by playing a more aggressive game than Lenglen had seen in her day. Lenglen, who was not used to losing games, and certainly not sets, began to assert herself in set two. She held service and broke Marble's third serve to go up 4-2. She took the second set and dominated through the third for the win.

First Round: Maureen Connolly over Althea Gibson: 6-3, 2-6, 6-3

"Little Mo's" baseline play and small stature came face-to-face with "Big Al's" serve and volley and her sheer size. Mo came out hitting junk and kept Gibson off balance, taking a 6-3 first set. The second set was won by Gibson's big serve. Little Mo broke Al's service four times in set three, but lost two of her own. Her consistent baseline returns gave her a 6-3 set and the match.

First Round: Helen Wills Moody over Margaret Smith Court: 6-4, 5-7, 6-4

The third straight matchup of baseline vs. the serve and volley technique had an added twist. Helen Moody's baseline game also included a big serve, making her a strong threat. The two players struggled against each other in an almost totally even match. In set one trailing 4-5 and at deuce, Court double-faulted and then lost the next point and the set. In set two, at 5-5, Moody hit two ground-strokes long and lost the game. Court served out the set 7-5 to draw even. Moody broke Court's second serve in set three. Moody forged ahead 3-1 and, playing even, held on for a 6-4 win.

First Round: Chris Evert Lloyd over Billie Jean King: 6-4, 4-6, 6-4.

Lloyd's baseline play met up with King's scrappy "Total game" many times during their careers. In this meeting, the points were long and bitterly fought as control passed back and forth. King tried to press the action in set three, but she lost to Lloyd's more deliberate, nearly error-free play. Serving at 4-3 in set three, Lloyd survived 10 deuce points to go up 5-3. She held on to win the match.

Semifinal: Suzanne Lenglen over Maureen Connolly: 1-6, 6-3, 6-3

During her career, Lenglen's weak serve normally did not prohibit her from going to the net. But would Connolly's firm, deep baseline strokes keep her back in this clash of diverse styles? Lenglen played cautiously in set one and lost to Connolly's powerful ground strokes. Changing tactics, Lenglen went to the net to take the next two sets with relative ease. Most amazing was the way Lenglen won, with accurate placements and an economy of points. She seldom had to play long games and seemed able to control the match from the second set on.

Semifinal: Helen Moody over Chris Evert Lloyd: 10-8, 3-6, 9-7

Two master baseliners squared off for a tough test. In an extremely long first set, Moody hit hard and deep, and Lloyd matched her stroke-for-stroke. Slightly more accurate, Moody finally pulled out the first set. Apparently letting up, she lost the second set. The stage was set for another long set, played from the baseline. Moody finally won, not by sparkling play, but by sheer endurance. It appeared that Lloyd had the ability to beat Moody, and might have done so had she varied her attack by running her opponent more. By staying on the baseline, Lloyd created a near stand-off that Moody won by the slimmest of margins.

Final: Suzanne Lenglen over Helen Moody: 6-4, 3-6, 10-8

The all-time finals offered an interesting contrast between the acrobatic Lenglen, who played the net without possessing a big serve, versus the less mobile Moody, who had a big serve but who stayed on the baseline after hitting it. In the tournament, Lenglen had shown a tendency to fall behind while learning her opponents' styles, and then to defeat them rather easily. She had not had to play a long match. It remained to be seen whether she could endure an extended match with many long points. The match offered an added attraction; it was a rematch of their sole meeting in Cannes, which Lenglen had won when Moody was only nineteen years old.

Learning a lesson about baseliners from the Connolly match, Lenglen went to the net from the start and took the first set. Moody came back to win the second set. The strength of her big serve overcame Lenglen's net play. Each won and lost using their strengths, and the stage was set for the final set between the two best. Each broke service once up to 6-6. At this point, Lenglen began running Moody up and back, and, at 8-8, Lenglen had slowed her down considerably. She held service at 9-8, and broke the exhausted Moody to win the championship. Moody—who had won two long sets from the baseline against Lloyd in the tournament's longest match—faltered when she had to move, and bowed out. The three baseline players had made the final four, but Lenglen emerged the victor. Even in the final match, there was a question as to whether Lenglen had been thoroughly tested, and whether she was physically superior or merely had outsmarted her opponents.

The triumph of Suzanne Lenglen in the All-Time Women's Tennis Tournament puts her in the company of some of the best stars in modern sports history. As the tournament's oldest participant, she demonstrated that old-timers can compete with and defeat modern players. Although not a big server, her aggressive net play carried her to victory over the strong baseline players, who seemed to dominate the tournament.

Lenglen and Moody slugged it out in the finals, using contrasting styles. The 18 game final set turned out to be a classic struggle. One style did not defeat the other. Lenglen found a slight weakness in Moody's mobility, and used it to wear her down. In the end, no player emerged as totally dominant. But tennis is a game of subtle differences. Lenglen found the edge she needed and took the all-time grass title. On clay, or under different tournament circumstances, another winner might have been possible. But on grass, in this all-time competition, Suzanne Lenglen is the all-time best.

The All-Time 100-Meter Dash

The Field

Don't blink or you'll miss it. Here it is—the fastest major sports event of all. Whereas other events may take several months, an hour, or a mere minute, this one is over in ten quick ticks of the clock.

Listed in historical order are the world's premier speed-burners with their country, best year, Olympic gold medal year, and fastest 100-meter and 100-yard times during the career of each.

Entry and Country	Best Year	Olympic Medal Year	Best 100 M.	Best 100 Yd.
Charles Paddock, U.S.	1921	1920	10.4 R	9.6 T
Eddie Tolan, U.S.	1929	1932	10.3 T	9.5 T
Ralph Metcalfe, U.S.	1934	None	10.3 T	Unknown
Jesse Owens, U.S.	1936	1936	10.2 R	9.4
Harrison Dillard, U.S.	1948	1948	10.3	Unknown
Melvin Patton, U.S.	1948	None	Unknown	9.3 R
Amin Hary, Germany	1960	1960	10.0 R	Unknown
Bob Hayes, U.S.	1964	1964	10.0 T	9.1 R
Henry Jerome, Canada	1966	None	10.0 T	9.1 T
Jim Hines, U.S.	1968	1968	9.95 R	9.1 T
Valeri Borzov, U.S.S.R.	1972	1972	10.1	Unknown
Ivory Crockett, U.S.	1974	None	9.9 T	9.0 R
Steve Williams, U.S.	1974	None	9.9 T	9.1 T
Houston McTear, U.S.	1975	None	Unknown	9.0 T
Hasely Crawford, Trinidad	1976	1976	10.1	Unknown

(R—broke world record, T—tied world record)

A certain amount of glamour surrounds the world's fastest runners. There is Jesse Owens, who gained international recognition in the 1936 Berlin Olympics by winning four gold medals. Adolph Hitler, a spectator at the Games, was so insulted by a black man single-handedly destroying his distorted belief in Aryan supremacy, that he left the stadium to avoid the embarrassment of having to receive the victorious Owens. Another entrant, Bob Hayes, successfully made the transition from Olympic sprinter to professional football player, and enjoyed many outstanding seasons with the Dallas Cowboys. Finally, Valeri Borzov of the U.S.S.R. scientifically studied sprinting, and earned a Ph.D. in physical culture by writing his doctoral dissertation on "the start" of the 100-meter dash.

But the All-Time 100-Meter Dash will not be won by glamour. The race will be run on the basis of the athletes' past performances on the cinder paths.

Nine of the fifteen entrants won a gold medal in the Olympics. None, however, were able to repeat their Olympic victory. Six of the Olympic gold medalists broke the world record in either the 100-meter or 100-yard dash. Paddock, Owens, Hary, and Hines set new marks in the 100-meter dash; Tolan and Hayes established new records over the 100-yard distance. Two non-winners in Olympic competition, Patton and Crockett, also broke the 100-yard record. Jim Hines is the only member of the field who broke the world record in the Olympic Games. He performed the feat in 1968 when many records fell in the light air of Mexico City.

Only three runners in the field failed to tie or break a world record in either the 100-meter or 100-yard dash. The threesome—Dillard, Borzov, and Crawford—all managed, however, to register Olympic victories. Dillard, the world's number one hurdler who fell in the 1948 Olympic trials, entered the 100-meter event as an afterthought and defeated Patton in the finals.

Surprisingly, among all these record-setting performances, no runner broke *both* the 100-meter and 100-yard
marks. Six of the sprinters, however, broke one record and
tied the other. Of the six, only Ivory Crockett failed to win in
the Olympics. The remaining five—Paddock, Tolan,
Owens, Hayes, and Hines—each won an Olympic gold
medal and broke or tied a world record. These runners
represent the class of the all-time field.

Of these top five, Charles Paddock stands out as an unusually superior runner in his day, but one who would probably
be outclassed by later sprinters. He won the Olympics back in
1920 and is the oldest runner in the field. In his peak, he tied
the 100-yard dash record of 9.6 seconds on six separate
occasions. In the Olympics, his 10.8 time for the 100 meters
fell short of the 10.6 record. The following year, however, he
shattered the world record with a time of 10.4. Paddock's
Olympic performance was way off his record time of the
following year. This may reflect his inability to excel in the
pressure events. Paddock's seven records set or tied, however, leads Tolan (4), Steve Williams (4, all ties), and Owens
and Hines (3 each).

Of the remaining top four, Tolan's 10.3 tied the world
record in 1932, Hayes equalled the world record with a time
of 10.0 in 1964, and Hines's 9.95 broke the world mark in
1968. These were all outstanding performances in Olympic
competition. Of the four premier sprinters, only Owens
failed to run at a record pace in the Olympic Games. His 10.3
was one-tenth of a second off the world record that he himself
held. It was a record that was to stand for twenty years, the
most enduring mark ever set by an Olympic dash winner.

The runners are preparing to take their marks in the starting
blocks. Who do you think will win? Will it be someone from
the distant past like Paddock or Tolan, who were often
clocked near world record times? Will it be a modern runner
like Crockett or McTear who recorded faster times under

improved conditions? Or will it be someone from the middle period—Owens, who held the world record, twenty years, Hayes, who tied the world record in the 1964 Olympics, or Hines, the only man to break a world record in this event under the pressure of the Olympic Games? The starter's gun is up and poised. The All-Time 100-Meter Dash is set to begin.

The Race

Hayes, Borzov, and McTear broke quickly from their starting blocks and sprang into a slim lead. Twenty meters down the track, Owens sprinted into first place followed by an onrushing Tolan and Hines. Owens, Tolan, and Hines were a blur of blinding speed as they raced for the finish line. The threesome leaned forward as they crossed the tape. Owens was a narrow victor in a thrilling photo finish. Tolan trailed in second by a hundredth of a second. Hines was third by the same split-second margin.

Hayes, who had broken on top at the start of the race, edged Dillard and Crawford in another photo finish for fourth. Dillard took fifth over Crawford. Both runners were clocked at 10.16.

A step back were Borzov, Paddock, and Crockett. McTear faded and was tucked into the field along with Metcalfe. Hary, Williams, Patton, and Jerome trailed.

Presented below is the final order of finish in the All-Time 100-Meter Dash:

1. Jesse Owens   10.09
2. Eddie Tolan   10.10
3. Jim Hines   10.11
4. Bob Hayes   10.15
5. Harrison Dillard   10.16
6. Hasely Crawford   10.16
7. Valeri Borzov   10.21

8.	Charles Paddock	10.22
9.	Ivory Crockett	10.23
10.	Ralph Metcalfe	10.26
11.	Houston McTear	10.26
12.	Amin Hary	10.30
13.	Steve Williams	10.31
14.	Melvin Patton	10.32
15.	Henry Jerome	10.44

The race was dominated by the Olympians, who took the first eight places. Jesse Owens' victory came as no real surprise considering his tremendous ability and record-setting accomplishments. Hines' and Hayes' high third and fourth place finishes, respectively, may be debated by some, but both men were truly great runners of the sixties. The biggest surprises of the race would have to be Eddie Tolan and Harrison Dillard. Tolan, a 1932 Olympics winner, lost to Owens by a mere hundredth of a second. Dillard, the 1948 Olympian, neither broke nor tied any records, but edged out the more recent Crawford and Borzov for a respectable fifth place finish.

With only two one-hundredths of a second separating the first three finishers, Owens, Tolan, and Hines all deserve accolades. But, even though it was by the very slimmest of margins, Jesse Owens emerged victorious as the fastest human being of all time.

The All-Time Mile Run

The Field

The mile run is one of the most celebrated events in all of sports. Rich in history, its major participants read like a "who's who" of track. Over the course of time, certain well-publicized matchups have been billed as "the dream mile." The All-Time Mile Run goes far beyond all these previous confrontations by bringing together in one race the greatest milers in track history.

This race will be as famous for the runners who are left out as for the ones who will compete. During the past years, the reduction in the world record time for the mile run has been so mathematically significant that many past great milers simply cannot compete with the modern distance runners. It was determined that a miler would have had to run consistently at a time of 3:55 or better to be selected for the all-time field.

Of the milers failing to qualify for this event, Finland's Paavo Nurmi is immediately conspicuous. Running from 1920 to 1931, Nurmi set 22 records at distances between one and thirteen miles. Winner of ten Olympic gold medals, his best time in the mile was 4:10.4.

In the thirties, Glenn Cunningham dominated the mile. "The Kansas Flash" introduced the strategy of running the second half of the mile faster than the first. Cunningham was clocked under 4:10 more than twenty times during his illustrious career. His best time was 4:06.7.

The early forties saw Arne Anderson and Gunder Hagg, both of Sweden, trade the mile record back and forth. Hagg also broke all long-distance records up to 5,000 meters. But Hagg is best known for his record 4:01.4 mile in 1945. His mark lasted nine years until Roger Bannister became the first man to break the four-minute barrier.

Nineteen fifty-four was an historic year for the mile event. First, Roger Bannister of England ran the first sub-four-minute mile in 3:59.4. Australian John Landy proceeded to break Bannister's record with a time of 3:58. In a special match race between these two great milers, Bannister won by passing Landy on the right when the Australian glanced back over his left shoulder.

All of these well-known milers who dominated the event of their day, failed to qualify for the All-Time Mile Run. For purposes of comparison, if any of today's 3:55 milers ran an *average* race and the old-timers recorded their *best* time, these old-timers would trail the 3:55 milers by the following margins: Landy, over 20 meters; Bannister, 33 meters; Hagg, 50 meters; Cunningham, 90 meters; and Nurvi, 115 meters.

The list of qualifiers for the All-Time Mile Run does include many prominent runners. The field is presented below in historical order:

Entry and Country	Best Year	Best Mile	Best 1,500 M.	Olympic Gold Medal Year
Herb Elliott, Australia	1960	3.545 R	3.35.6 R	1960 R
Peter Snell, New Zealand	1962	3.54.1 R	unknown	1964
Jim Ryun, U.S.	1967	3.51.1 R	3.33.1 R	none
Kip Keino, Kenya	1967	3.53.1	3.34.9	1968
Ben Jipcho, Kenya	1973	3.52.0	unknown	none
Filbert Bayi, Tanzania	1975	3.51.0 R	3.32.2 R	none
John Walker, New Zealand	1975	3.49.4 R	3.32.2	1976
Marty Liquori, U.S.	1975	3.52.2	3.36.0	none
Sebastian Coe, England	1979	3.48.95 R	3.32.1 R	1980

(R—Broke World Record)

The oldest qualifier, Herb Elliott, is probably the proto-type of the classic miler. Specializing in the mile run, he broke both the mile and 1,500-meter records in 1958. Elliott is the only runner in the all-time field and one of the only two-milers in history to break the 1,500-meter record in the Olympics. He held the 1,500-meter record for an unprece-dented nine years.

Peter Snell is better known as a half-miler. He won the 800 meters in the 1960 Olympics before moving up to the mile two years later. Snell broke records in the 800 meters, 880 yards, and the mile in 1962. In the 1964 Olympic Games, he fashioned an 800 and 1,500-meter double win. It was the first time since 1920 this feat had been accomplished.

Jim Ryun, the premier American miler, ran more great miles than anyone but Kip Keino. Ryun held the mile world record for nine years, tying Gunder Hagg for the longest reign in modern times. More impressive was the American's 1,500-meter world record time of 3.31.1 in 1967. After breaking the mark that had stood for seven years, Ryun's own record stood for seven years. This achievement virtually places Ryun in a class by himself. He had a disappointing loss to Keino in the '68 Olympics.

Kenyans Kip Keino and Ben Jipcho were known for dis-tances longer than the mile. Although both were fast pace setters, they never held records in the mile run or the 1,500 meters. Keino broke the 3,000 meter record and Jipcho the 3,000 meter Steeplechase record. Keino ran many miles under 3.58 and beat Ryun in the '68 Olympics.

Along with Elliott and Ryun, Filbert Bayi held both the mile run and 1,500 meter records. A torrid pace setter, he broke Ryun's long-standing mile record but lost it to Walker in the same year, 1975.

John Walker brought a large muscular physique to the event often dominated by thinner runners. He became the world's fastest miler in 1975 but coasted to a slow Olympic win in 1976, when the major competition was not running.

Marty Liquori has never been the world's top miler. However, he has continued to improve his time through a long career and his best times qualify him to run with the all-time best.

Sebastian Coe broke the 800 meter and mile run records in 1979 within a two week period. He runs longer races, but considers the 800 meters his specialty.

The All-Time Mile shapes up as a tight race that any of the runners can win. It may appear that each runner will run his best time and that the very latest record breakers will be the favorites. But milers do not always run their best times. In fact, of the six record breakers in this field, only Elliott and Ryun improved on their records. More often, record breakers suffer some kind of psychological letdown and never do as well again. Often, too, records come on particular tracks where everything is just right. The same record breaker may not even win if the track is different or if the entire field of runners is strategy-wise and in peak condition.

Consistency over a long season or several seasons may mean more than one or two big performances which are never again duplicated. If consistency were the sole test, then Ryun and Keino would be the favorites.

The level of competition may serve to bring out the best in some runners. Elliott seemed to run against himself, beating his own world record in Olympic competition while going untested by the field. Walker ran poorly in the Olympics when he was untested. The pace-setting Kenyans seemed to run only hard enough to win.

Strategy and pacing may have much to do with the result of this race. Most of these milers have great finishing kicks and will save up for the right moment. Ryun and Walker are probably the strongest of the kickers. They will lay off of the pace, which will probably be set by either Keino, Jipcho, or Bayi. However, these pace-setters sometimes will drop off the pace and then pick it up again to break the rhythm of their opponents.

Will an unusual piece of strategy affect this race? The field is competitive. The pacers and sprinters are both well represented. Would anything be a surprise in such a field?

As the runners take their marks, who do you pick to win? Will it be an Olympic winner? A faster-timed modern record holder? An older runner who held the record a long time? One with a long career? A strategist?

The Race

At the gun, Jipcho and Keino bolted from the middle of the pack and took the lead. The field was bunched around the first turn, but as they came into the back stretch the Kenyans ran side-by-side in the lead. Snell and Bayi followed. Elliott, Liquori and Coe trailed by a few yards. Ryun and Walker brought up the rear. They held their position through the first lap, which was run in 58.0.

Midway through lap two, Coe began moving up fast. He was on Keino's shoulder at the end of the second lap. The others held their places. Keino's time at the midway point of the race was 1.56.2.

On the back stretch of lap three, Coe went to the front and opened up an eight yard lead on the field. Bayi passed the Kenyans to take over second. Ryun made a big move to fifth, with Elliott staying with him. Snell, Liquori, and Walker trailed. Ryun picked up ground to close in on Coe at lap's end. Elliott stayed with Ryun in third, with Bayi a close fourth. Coe's time after three laps was 2.53.4.

Excitement was in the air for the bell lap. Coming off the turn, Ryun, Elliott, and Bayi moved as a group past the leading Coe. Ryun had about a step on Elliott. Bayi held fast just another stride back.

In the back stretch, Walker started a charge from last place and pulled up even with Coe in the fourth position. Snell remained close in sixth as the others fell back.

Ryun continued his kick all the way to the finish line to win by about ten feet. Elliott held off a fast-charging Bayi to take second by about five feet. About ten yards back in fourth place was Coe, who held off both Walker's charge and the steady Snell by a few feet. Keino, Jipcho, and Liquori closed out the field. Ryun's winning time was a respectable 3.51.2, short of a record.

The Finish

Place	Entry	Country	Time
1	Jim Ryun	United States	3.51.2
2	Herb Elliott	Australia	3.51.6
3	Filbert Bayi	Tanzania	3.51.8
4	Sebastian Coe	England	3.53.1
5	John Walker	New Zealand	3.53.3
6	Peter Snell	New Zealand	3.53.6
7	Kip Keino	Kenya	3.55.4
8	Ben Jipcho	Kenya	3.55.9
9	Marty Liquori	United States	3.56.2

The All-Time Mile saw the Kenyans set the pace, Coe try to steal it early, and Ryun and Walker sprint at the end. Ryun, Bayi, and Coe finished well, as expected, with Ryun simply outkicking them for the victory. The big surprise was probably Elliott, the oldest entry, who moved with Ryun on his sprint and stayed a close second at the finish.

Jim Ryun ran a strong race, showing a blazing kick that set him apart. By a clear margin, Jim Ryun reigns as the greatest of history's all-time best milers.

The All-Time Decathlon

The Field

The winner of the Decathlon in the modern Olympics is usually labeled the best all-round athlete in the world. Whether or not this is true, no one will deny that the ten events-in-one represents one of the most grueling tests in all of sports. Each athlete must compete in ten running, jumping and throwing events over a period of two afternoons. The events, with some rest in between, can take eight hours or more. They end on the second day with the running of the 1,500 meters. If the participant is not tired or injured by then, the last event will certainly drain his remaining energy.

The Decathlon stands as a test of training and endurance. No one can win the Decathlon unless he completes all ten events. A contestant could conceivably win nine events, but not score in the tenth, and lose to every other opponent. Once a candidate shows he can complete the ten events, he needs to combine certain strengths in order to be a winning performer. Some candidates will do this by being balanced throughout most of the events. Jim Thorpe and Bruce Jenner were this type of athlete. Other Decathlon winners were quite unbalanced, such as Jim Bausch, who was strong in throwing events but a weak runner, or Bill Toomey who was weak in throwing but a good runner.

The candidates for the All-Time Decathlon are some of the greatest names in sports history. Here is a preview of the group who will compete for the title of the world's greatest athlete.

Jim Thorpe. Who has not heard of the legendary Jim Thorpe? He was a legend at Carlisle (PA) Indian Institute, for whom he scored 16 points in a football upset over Harvard. At another time, he headed a two-man track team that beat Lafayette. Born in Oklahoma, the 6′2″, 190 pound star lived 1888-1953. He won the 1912 Olympic Decathlon with a score good enough to have won in 1920 and 1924, as well. His margin was 592 points over Sweden's Hugo Wieslander. Stripped of his medals for semi-pro baseball activity, his amateur status was reinstated twenty years after his death. He showed no real weaknesses, and was strongest in the 100 meters, high jump and high hurdles. In one 1950 poll, he was voted the outstanding athlete of the first half of the twentieth century.

Jim Bausch. He was a 200-pound fireplug who plunged from fullback for the University of Kansas football team. He took up the decathlon, and, in the 1932 Olympics, upset Finnish world record holder Akilles Jarvinen. An unbalanced performer, he was weak in the running events but very strong in the shot put, discus, javelin, and the pole vault.

Glenn Morris. An automobile salesman from Fort Collins, Colorado, this 24-year-old won the 1936 Olympics and became the All American Boy. A balanced performer with a lanky body, he ran a great 1500 meters and led a one, two, three sweep of the event for the United States.

Bob Mathias. At age 18, he became the youngest Olympic winner after taking part in the 1948 games. He became the only repeat decathlon winner in 1952, for which he is rated for this all-time event. From an anemic child, he grew to be 6′2″ and 200 pounds, and became a football and track star at Tulare High School in California. Surprisingly, his first decathlon came just two months before his 1948 Olympic triumph. A balanced performer, his one weakness in this competition is his 1500 meters.

Rafer Johnson. Born in Hillsboro, Texas this 6′3″, 200

pounder qualified as a long jumper, and the decathlon favorite, while a UCLA student in 1956. A knee injury led to a second place decathlon finish behind fellow American Milt Campbell. Returning in 1960, Johnson outdueled UCLA teammate C.K. Yang who competed for Taiwan. The American lost 7 of the 10 events to Yang, but scored more points, a tribute to Johnson's overall balance.

Bill Toomey. Born in Philadelphia, this 6′1″, 195 pounder attended Worcester (Mass.) Academy and the University of Colorado. Originally a quarter miler and long jumper, he turned to the decathlon, but was edged out of the Olympic qualifying in 1964. Winning 24 of 28 decathlons in 1966-69, he edged out Hans-Joachim Walde of West Germany in the 1968 Olympics by 82 points, then went on to break the world record in 1969. Although strong in the 100, 400 and long jump, a severe cut of the right hand during his youth handicapped his throwing events.

Nicolai Avilov. This 6′3″, 181 pound Russian from the Ukraine participated in three Olympics. He did not place in 1968, but won in 1972 and returned for a third in 1976. He was strongest in the long jump, high jump, hurdles, and pole vault, and can be remembered for sprinting to the finish in the 1500 meters. Avilov broke the record while holding both sides in painful agony.

Bruce Jenner. This 6′2″, 194 pound native of Mount Kisco, N.Y. and Sandy Hook, Connecticut started preparation for winning the 1976 Olympics in 1972. Finishing tenth behind the winner Avilov, Jenner told him, ''Next time, I'm going to beat you.'' He trained for four years, and, peaking at the Olympics, broke Avilov's record. Sometimes called the best second day performer in history, he was a balanced performer with no apparent weak events. Although Jenner had five personal bests in the 1976 Olympics, his 1500 meters is his only standout event in this star-studded field.

What can be expected from this field of outstanding athletes? Obviously, no one will be a runaway winner. Some of the standouts may win three or four of the events, but the ultimate winner might be one who wins few of the individual events.

The Decathlon divides into two days of activity. The first day features speed in the 100 meters, long jump and 400 meters events. The shot put and high jump round out the day's activity.

Day two favors the throwers, with the discus and javelin on the same day. The pole vault adds another field event that, along with the high hurdles and the 1500 meters, makes this a difficult day for the speed candidates.

If things go as expected, Jim Thorpe and Bill Toomey should show well the first day. Thorpe is an automatic winner of the opening 100 meters, and the field will try to catch him during the rest of day one. Toomey will need to lead the field by 500 points on the first day to win, for he is the weakest second day performer.

Bruce Jenner has been called the best second day performer in history, but he faces stiff competition from Jim Bausch, who will dominate the discus and javelin and will be strong in the pole vault. Bausch, however, is probably too weak in the running events to win overall.

If the score is close after nine events, the 1500 meters could make the difference for Jenner, Morris, Avilov, or Thorpe, who all do it well.

Popular opinion suggests that Thorpe, Mathias, and Jenner may be the class of the field. All three are balanced performers, and, along with the somewhat unheralded but steady Glen Morris, should be considered the favorites. Mathias will need a big lead going into the 1500 to win. But the others are very competitive in that event, and the whole Decathlon may come down to the last event.

An interesting comparison emerges in this matchup of the all-time great decathlon stars. The oldest performer, Jim

Thorpe, competed in 1912, while the latest, Jenner, won in 1976. The 64-year time frame of the various performers creates both problems and possibilities. If judged simply by who has done the best in the total events, then the last performer would be the best, the next to last would be second, and so forth.

However, if performers are compared by their performance times, then the results may be quite different. For example, in the 100 meters, Toomey has the best actual time (10.4) and Thorpe has the worst (11.2). Should Toomey be considered the best and Thorpe the worst based on their actual performances without regard for improved conditions and different methods of training? Consider that Thorpe ran his 11.2 when 10.8 won the Olympic best in that event. Toomey ran his 10.4 when 9.9 won the Olympics. By this method of comparison, Thorpe looks better. If a similar comparison is made in each of the events, then a possible objective evaluation can be made across the 64-year time period.

Judging by this more objective standard, the favorites for each event, in order of ranking, are as follows:

100 meters: Thorpe, Mathias, Toomey
Long jump: Toomey, Johnson, Avilov, Mathias, Bausch
Shot put: Bausch, Mathias, Morris, Thorpe
High jump: Thorpe, Avilov, Mathias
400 meters: Toomey, Morris, Jenner
High hurdles: Thorpe, Morris, Toomey, Mathias
Discus: Bausch, Morris, Mathias, Johnson, Thorpe
Pole vault: Bausch, Mathias, Jenner, Johnson
Javelin: Bausch, Johnson, Mathias
1,500 meters: Jenner, Morris, Avilov, Thorpe

Using this as a guide, you now can make an educated guess as to who will win the all-time Decathlon. Remember that balance through the ten events is the best way to win in the complicated point system. Although Thorpe, Toomey, and Bausch look like the big individual winners, that does not guarantee victory. The contestants who appear to be favorites in the most events are Mathias (8), Thorpe (6), Morris (5) and Bausch (5). With this information before you, decide now who is the all-time best athlete. The competition is about to begin.

The Events

Day 1: All-Time Decathlon

100 Meters. Jim Thorpe got off to his expected lead by winning with a time of 10.43. His 951 points topped Mathias with 10.54 (920 points) and Toomey 10.57 (912.5 points).

Long Jump. Bill Toomey, as most expected, took first with 26′ 6.22″ (1036 points). Johnson, Avilov, Mathias, Bausch, and Thorpe were all close. After two events, the leaders were: 1. Toomey 1948.5, 2. Mathias 1879, 3. Thorpe 1863.

Shot Put. Strong man Jim Bausch took the event with a 66′ 6.85″ (1081 points). Mathias, Morris, Thorpe, and Johnson kept pace. After three events it was 1. Mathias 2872, 2. Thorpe 2811, 3. Johnson 2757.5.

High Jump. It was another strong event for Thorpe who did 7′ 1.58″ (1002 points) and took a slight lead over Mathias. Avilov and Mathias also showed well. After four events: 1. Thorpe 3813, 2. Mathias 3806. Five others all bunched closely in the 3500's and Jenner trailed the field.

400 Meters. Bill Toomey took his second event with a time of 46.08 (996 points). Morris, Johnson, Jenner and Thorpe were next in order.

First Day Decathlon Totals, Five Events

1.	Thorpe	4,718
2.	Mathias	4,686

3.	Morris	4,542.5
4.	Toomey	4,502.5
5.	Johnson	4,466.5
6.	Avilov	4,426
7.	Jenner	4,298
8.	Bausch	4,250.5

After the first day, the running of Thorpe and Toomey stood out. But Toomey's disappointing fourth place had eliminated him, for he is the weakest second day performer. Bausch's and Jenner's strong overall abilities should raise them on day two, but they appear too far back to win. It looks like the balanced performance of Thorpe, Mathias, and Morris will carry them through, but Mathias will be weak in the concluding 1500 meters.

Day 2: All-Time Decathlon

110-Meter High Hurdles. Jim Thorpe put himself in good shape for the overall title by taking the hurdles in 13.74 (994 points). Morris, Toomey and Mathias also had good times. The leaders remained the same after six events: 1. Thorpe 5712, 2. Mathias 5616, 3. Morris 5508.5.

Discus Throw. Jim Bausch took his expected discus win with 199' 5.38" (1052 points). But the excitement was with the leaders who stayed bunched, and held their first three places. After seven events it was: 1. Thorpe 6670, 2. Mathias 6614, 3. Morris 6506.5.

Pole Vault. Bob Mathias was surprised when Jim Bausch took the event with 16' 8.73" (1074 points). However, Mathias beat Thorpe by 77 points, and for the first time since the third event, took a 21 point lead with two events to go. Leading the rest of the field by about 200 points, these two appeared to fight each other for the all-time title. With Thorpe expected to be much better in the 1500 meters, Mathias had to build up a big lead in the javelin in order to hold off Thorpe. After eight events the leaders were: 1. Mathias 7628, 2. Thorpe 7607, 3. Morris 7420.5.

Final Results

	Jim Thorpe 1912	Jim Bausch 1932	Glenn Morris 1936	Bob Mathias 1952	Rafer Johnson 1960	Bill Toomey 1968	Nicolai Avilov 1972	Bruce Jenner 1976
100 M.	10.43	11.43	10.84	10.54	10.75	10.57	10.9	10.94
	951	702.5	845	920	867.5	912.5	830	810
Long Jump	24'5.38"	24'10.87"	23'8.09"	25'2.84"	25'7.439"	26'6.22"	25'6.229"	23'8.2"
	912	939	864	959	982	1036	976	865
Shot Put	58'4.98"	66'6.85"	60'5.70'	61'1.56"	55'10.938"	46'6.62"	47'1.97"	50'4.2"
	948	1081	984.5	993	908	741	753	809
High Jump	7'1.58"	6'4.38"	6'8.64"	6'10.36"	6'3.746"	6'4.97"	7'0.21"	6'8"
	1002	804	899	934	789	817	970	882
400 M.	47.93	51.92	47.02	48.41	47.61	46.08	48.07	47.51
	905	724	950	880	920	996	897	923
1st Day Totals	4,718	4,250.5	4,542.5	4,686	4,466.5	4,502.5	4,426	4,298
	1	8	3	2	5	4	6	7

	Jim Thorpe 1912	Jim Bausch 1932	Glenn Morris 1936	Bob Mathias 1952	Rafer Johnson 1960	Bill Toomey 1968	Nicolai Avilov 1972	Bruce Jenner 1976
110 High Hurdles	13.74 / 994	14.76 / 874	13.96 / 966	14.27 / 930	14.746 / 875	14.09 / 951	14.37 / 918	14.84 / 866
Discus	180'8.28" / 958	199'5.38" / 1052	188'7.42" / 998	188'7.91" / 998	181'5.24" / 962	149'5.65" / 792	161'6.8" / 858	164'2" / 871
Pole Vault	14'9.85" / 937	16'8.73" / 1074	14'6.22" / 914	14'10.23" / 1014	15'8.579" / 1004	14'0.61" / 879	14'11.25" / 945	15'9" / 1008
Javelin	233'9.156" / 894	264'2.96" / 996	234'5.48" / 897	249'0.95" / 945	255'9.68" / 967	216'4.05" / 833	211'6.24" / 814	224'10" / 862
1500 M.	4:28.23 / 601	5:00.5 / 407.5	4:22.9 / 640.5	4:43.0 / 505	4:51.12 / 459	5:03.0 / 390	4:26.29 / 615	4:12.61 / 714
[Total Points]	9,102	8,654	8,958	9,078	8,733.5	8,347.5	8,576	8,618
[Place]	1	5	3	2	4	8	7	6

Javelin. Bausch won the event, his third of the day, with a toss of 264' 2.96" (996 points). Mathias finished third, but the important thing was the points he gained on Thorpe. Adding only 51 points to his lead on Thorpe, he led by a mere 72 points with the 1500 meters to go. Mathias needed to stay within about 12 seconds of Thorpe's 1500 meters time to maintain his lead, and that seemed unlikely. After nine events the leaders were: 1. Mathias 8573, 2. Thorpe 8501, 3. Morris 8317.5.

1500 Meters. The event that can make or break a great decathlon brought out a new winner. Bruce Jenner won in 4.12.61 (714 points), and moved from eighth to sixth place in the finals. However, the big news was Jim Thorpe, who ran fourth behind Jenner, Avilov and Morris, and beat Bob Mathias by nearly 15 seconds. By a mere 24 points, Jim Thorpe overhauled the second day challenge of Bob Mathias and became the all-time champ. Mathias finished a strong second, and Glenn Morris was a very able third. The others trailed by larger margins.

Congratulations go to Jim Thorpe for winning the All-Time Decathlon. In doing so, he establishes himself as perhaps the greatest athlete ever. He was truly a remarkable performer.

Afterword

Computers have been used to evaluate many sports events during the last 20 years. Four of these received media attention, and are well known. In 1967, Miami promoter Murray Woroner utilized an NCR-315 to stage a heavyweight boxing tournament. Rocky Marciano defeated Jack Dempsey in the finals. In 1968, Woroner repeated the event for the middleweights, with Ray Robinson defeating Stanley Ketchel in the finals. In 1968, Radio Station WIOD staged an All-Time Horse Race, which Citation won. Man o' War ran second. In 1970, NBC ran an eight team Baseball Playoff, in which the 1927 Yankees defeated the 1961 Yankees in the finals.

Each of these attempts exhibited flaws, which an expert in sports data analysis should be able to observe and correct. For example, Marciano was the only undefeated boxer in the heavyweight tournament. Although boxing experts generally rate him no better than fifth or sixth best all-time, his undefeated record against meager opposition was apparently used to sway the result in his favor.

The WIOD Horse Race favored class, weight-carrying ability, and the overall record over speed records, margins of victory and total earnings. Another selection process could have changed drastically the results.

The NBC Baseball Playoff involved the selection of eight teams by a panel of six ''experts,'' including Ted Williams, Stan Musial, Joe DiMaggio and Willie Mays. They obviously are not research experts. That playoff also limited each matchup to one game rather than a series of games, as baseball actually is played. The 1927 Yankees were crowned the best in history on the basis of winning only three games, and Waite Hoyt pitched all three. Such a handling of the sport, and the multitude of possibilities that could occur over a long series, oversimplified the project to the point of absurdity.

Computer matchups will continue to be made in the area of sport. However, all such matchups are not necessarily based on the best research and analysis available. The vast amount of research that has been done in all areas of the sports world is unknown to most sports fans. Without attempting to detail all of this activity, a framework will be presented that allows accurate research and analysis. This framework was used for most of the sports research done for this book.

Four things are needed to properly evaluate the best in any sport: (1) data, (2) interpretation of data, (3) a replay structure, and (4) a significant statistical sampling.

An objective observer is needed to record the original data or information. When reading old newspaper accounts in some sports, one is treated to more opinion than data. Boxers and tennis players are often "great," or "clearly inferior," with no information to support the opinion. Two sports that have kept good records throughout their history are baseball and horse racing. Documentation includes box scores, in which were recorded several categories of data, not just the final result.

More recently, such sports as hockey and basketball have added new categories of information, which aids analysis of today's teams, but which are lacking when old teams are analyzed. Some sports have gone through re-evaluations. *The Baseball Encyclopedia*, 1969, actually changed some of the official statistics of baseball history by going back and recounting all of the old box scores. The continuing project, *Data Boxing*, has introduced new categories in boxing statistics, by using films to count every blow thrown in the major bouts of boxing history.

This kind of research activity will continue to be applied to more sports. The ultimate goal is total information. Obviously, this goal is more possible in some sports than in others, but it remains the researcher's dream.

Collecting data is not enough. One cannot simply total up the results and determine the all-time best. The data must be interpreted, and that requires mathematical formulas.

Computers should be seen for what they are in this process. Computers don't make up interpretations—usually called programs. People make up the programs and put them in the computer. The computer does what it is told. People, then, must make the interpretive evaluations. The computer is simply a large adding machine for totalling up what people have decided by their interpretations.

How can we properly interpret the data of the best sports performers?

Sports fans will often talk of an undefeated career or the longest career, the longest reign as champ or the longest win streak, the most of this or the least of that. Such issues are interesting, but often oversimplify and don't do justice to the entire range of the sport. Fans frequently judge by only one item of data, often the final result, and forget hundreds of other items that may outweigh it. For example, a perfect career of final results for a boxer does not denote a perfect boxer on the whole range of data. There is no boxer who is perfect on all items such as knockdowns, cuts, TKOs, rounds won, and blows scored.

Claims of superiority based on any one event are also meaningless. All sports performers do have a big day, but not all are consistent over a season or a series of big matches.

The most objective standard seems to be the evaluation of team sports on the basis of their best regular season, and individual sports performers on their peak periods.

For evaluating team sports, the regular season works better than the playoffs, for a greater amount of data is accumulated. Furthermore, all teams participate in the regular season. Comparisons can be made more easily in leagues, which exist as a closed system with the same number of games for each.

Individual performance sports are usually not subject to seasonal limits and are more properly evaluated by considering the peak period of each. Each sport has its unique features, but generally, a peak should last from three to seven years. It should begin when competition begins against major opposition and continue until the performer declines in ability or goes into a long retirement. Not only should the performer be evaluated, but his opponents should be evaluated. No performance exists in a vacuum. It must be seen in relation to a time, a series of events, and against a certain level of opposition.

Once the peak period is determined for the individual or the peak season for a team, then that performance must be evaluated using all the data that is available. In some sports that may require up to 200 variables or cateories of data. It is these variables that must be interpreted by use of elaborate formulas.

At times the data will be allowed to exist as pure numbers. Sometimes they will be converted to percentages. A common method of interpretation is to compare a statistic to the league average, or to the average for the history of the sport. Combinations of each of these are also possible.

When there are many variables operating in an individual sport, such as in boxing or tennis, a tree of variables may be needed. In other words, some variables will be judged as more important and that will be indicated in the formulas. Again, it may be advisable to let the variables operate independently, in which case no stair-step of values will be made, and randomness will determine what happens.

The process of normalization has revolutionized sports data analysis. Introduced in Jack Kavanagh's *Extra Innings*

(3d Ed.), the concept allows for the meeting of sports contestants and teams that competed at different points in history.

The process requires an extra step of data interpretation which most analysts have not considered. In team sports, it involves comparing statistics from various eras in a sport's history to the same point in time. For example, when Babe Ruth hit 60 home runs in 1927, they represented .137 of the total league production. When Roger Maris broke Ruth's record by hitting 61, in 1961, his production represented .04 of the league total. In normalization, both of these would be compared to a standard somewhere between the two. The result would be that Maris' rating would be somewhat reduced, while Ruth's would probably be raised. A similar operation would be used for each of perhaps 100 significant categories in the sport. Only then would an objective standard be possible for a proper historical analysis of a sport.

Once the data of a sport has been assembled and interpreted, it should be used in a replay structure. Computers or simulation games, which use dice, spinners, or random numbers, make it possible to replay historical events or create hypothetical matchups. Such a replay structure can go a long way toward establishing the all-time best in any sport.

Even though a sports figure's data has been interpreted in his ratings, that does not tell his full story. The properly rated performer must compete at a certain place, under specific conditions, against specific opposition, and within a consistent framework of rules and rule interpretations. The home field, rain, a strict official, two-platooning, or a bout shortened to ten rounds, are all variable conditions that can affect a result. The replay structure should allow for a variety of conditions. However, any all-time playoff should maintain a consistency of conditions throughout the competition.

In any simulated matchup, using a computer or a game, decisions must be made about style of play. Should the quarterback run or pass? Should the server crash the net or stay in back court? Must the performer employ his usual style, or may he switch styles if it is to his advantage? Some performers have several styles of play, while others have but one. Will the matchup allow complex strategy and tactics, or will these be simple and programmed into the structure? If the strategy is complex, then a person must interact with the replay for each performer, i.e., act as his brain, and make decisions for him. Computer tournaments often leave out this vital, personal element.

In the playoffs in this project, conditions have been carefully controlled for consistency. Whenever possible, personal involvement with the replay was maintained, to insure the ability to take advantage of every opportunity. In the more complex team sports, the personal coaching principle was scrupulously adhered to. The replay structure gave opportunity for maximum success of every contestant in the project.

After the data, the interpretation, and the conditions have been determined, the remaining need is for a significant statistical sample. This means that there must be enough results to establish a clear pattern.

The number of results may vary from one sport to another. Baseball, with fewer actual individual events within one game, may need a long playoff system, such as is used in the major leagues. Football, with an average of 120 plays per game, may need only one game to determine which is the best of two teams.

Team sports, which have their overall ability spread out over a number of players, will require longer playoffs than individual sports to determine who is best. The complex interworking of the various parts would seem to demand a larger sampling to insure that the overall trend has indeed been established. Conversely, individual sports may be evaluated by a small sample. In fact, individual sports which keep a lot of data, such as boxing, tennis and horse racing, may be the most manageable for achieving significant results.

For the purposes of this project, the playoff practices of each particular sport were used. Baseball uses a series; so did this project. Football uses a single game; the project followed suit.

However, all the results given here represent a trend of a much larger series of results. All the contestants, in all the sports, participated in many matchups, with most of the other competition in their sport. These results are a compendium of the most significant matchups in each sport.

No result represents a chance occurrence. They are all reliable results, based on the best data analysis available in the sport world.

Some of the playoffs, such as in baseball and boxing, are based on thousands of results. Obviously, no one person could have completed all of the replay of the matchups. The authors wish to pay their respects to all those simulation players, who, by use of computers or games, helped to make this possible. If you ever sent in an all-time playoff result to any game journal, you had a part in this project.

Recommended Games:

Of the hundreds of games on the market, the authors recommend, without reservation, the following games for playing with the all-time greats.

APBA Golf
  APBA Game Co., Box 1447, Lancaster, PA, 17604.

Data Boxing
  BLM Game Co., 321 East Superior St., Duluth, Minnesota, 55802.

Extra Innings (Baseball)
Real Life Basketball

Gamecraft Co., Box 2299, Station A, Champaign, Illinois, 61820.

Speculative Hockey Explorations
Arnold Kalnitsky, 7792 Kildare Rd., Montreal, Quebec, H4W1C5.

Statis-Pro Basketball (Professional)
Track Meet (Decathlon)
Avalon Hill, 4517 Haverford Rd., Baltimore, MD, 21214.

Strat-O-Matic Baseball
Strat-O-Matic Game Co., 46 Railroad Plaza, Glen Head, N.Y., 11545.

The Thoroughbred Racing Game
Vic Hasselblad, 8805 Boar's Head Court, Raleigh, N.C., 27612.

TEMPO BOOKS

SPORTS

BIOGRAPHIES

Get all the facts on your favorite superstars—complete career records plus a look at the personal side of today's top names in sports.